JOHN CALVIN (1509–1564)

"The Soul of Life":
The Piety of John Calvin

Introduced and Edited by
Joel R. Beeke

Reformation Heritage Books
Grand Rapids, Michigan

The Soul of Life
© 2009 by Joel R. Beeke

Published by
Reformation Heritage Books
2965 Leonard St., NE
Grand Rapids, MI 49525
616-977-0599 / Fax: 616-285-3246
e-mail: orders@heritagebooks.org
website: www.heritagebooks.org

All Scripture quotations are from Calvin's own translation or from
the Holy Bible, King James Version.

Library of Congress Cataloging-in-Publication Data

Calvin, Jean, 1509-1564.
  The soul of life : the piety of John Calvin / introduced & edited by
Joel R. Beeke.
      p. cm. -- (Profiles in reformed spirituality)
  Includes bibliographical references.
  ISBN 978-1-60178-057-7 (pbk. : alk. paper)
  1. Piety. 2. Christian life. 3. Spiritual life. 4. Calvin, Jean,
1509-1564. 5. Calvinism. 6. Reformed Church--Doctrines. I. Beeke,
Joel R., 1952- II. Title.
  BV4647.P5C35 2009
  248.4'842--dc22
                                        2009000562

---

*For additional Reformed literature, both new and used, request a free book
list from Reformation Heritage Books at the above address.*

With gratitude to

Esther Idelette Beeke

my beautiful, obedient daughter,
my avid reader and diligent student,
and my efficient employee—
you are your father's delight.

Enjoy these selections from the husband
of your namesake.
(Idelette was the God-fearing wife of John Calvin.)

Soli Deo Gloria!

PROFILES IN REFORMED SPIRITUALITY

series editors—Joel R. Beeke and Michael A. G. Haykin

Table of Contents

Section Five: Practical Dimensions

Profiles in Reformed Spirituality

Charles Dickens' famous line in *A Tale of Two Cities*—
"it was the best of times, it was the worst of times"
—seems well suited to western Evangelicalism since
the 1960s. On the one hand, these decades have seen
much for which to praise God and to rejoice. In His
goodness and grace, for instance, Reformed truth is
no longer a house under siege. Growing numbers
identify themselves theologically with what we hold
to be biblical truth, namely, Reformed theology and
piety. And yet, as an increasing number of Reformed
authors have noted, there are many sectors of the
surrounding western Evangelicalism that are charac-
terized by great shallowness and a trivialization of the
weighty things of God. So much of Evangelical worship seems barren. And when it comes to spirituality,
there is little evidence of the riches of our heritage as
Reformed Evangelicals.

As it was at the time of the Reformation, when the
watchword was *ad fontes*—"back to the sources"—so
it is now: the way forward is backward. We need to
go back to the spiritual heritage of Reformed Evangelicalism to find the pathway forward. We cannot
live in the past; to attempt to do so would be anti-
quarianism. But our Reformed forebearers in the faith
can teach us much about Christianity, its doctrines,
its passions, and its fruit.

And they can serve as our role models. As R. C. Sproul has noted of such giants as Augustine, Martin Luther, John Calvin, and Jonathan Edwards: "These men all were conquered, overwhelmed, and spiritually intoxicated by their vision of the holiness of God. Their minds and imaginations were captured by the majesty of God the Father. Each of them possessed a profound affection for the sweetness and excellence of Christ. There was in each of them a singular and unswerving loyalty to Christ that spoke of a citizenship in heaven that was always more precious to them than the applause of men."[1]

To be sure, we would not dream of placing these men and their writings alongside the Word of God. John Jewel (1522–1571), the Anglican apologist, once stated: "What say we of the fathers, Augustine, Ambrose, Jerome, Cyprian?... They were learned men, and learned fathers; the instruments of the mercy of God, and vessels full of grace. We despise them not, we read them, we reverence them, and give thanks unto God for them. Yet...we may not make them the foundation and warrant of our conscience: we may not put our trust in them. Our trust is in the name of the Lord."[2]

Seeking then both to honor the past and yet not idolize it, we are issuing these books in the series Profiles in Reformed Spirituality. The design is to introduce the spirituality and piety of the Reformed

---

1. "An Invaluable Heritage," *Tabletalk*, 23, no. 10 (October 1999): 5–6.

2. Cited in Barrington R. White, "Why Bother with History?" *Baptist History and Heritage*, 4, no. 2 (July 1969): 85.

tradition by presenting descriptions of the lives of notable Christians with select passages from their works. This combination of biographical sketches and collected portions from primary sources gives a taste of the subjects' contributions to our spiritual heritage and some direction as to how the reader can find further edification through their works. It is the hope of the publishers that this series will provide riches for those areas where we are poor and light of day where we are stumbling in the deepening twilight.

—Joel R. Beeke
Michael A. G. Haykin

Abbreviations and
Acknowledgments

The selections from Calvin in this volume are taken from the following books:

Commentary — *Commentaries of Calvin.* 46 vols. Various translators. Edinburgh: Calvin Translation Society, 1843–55; reprint ed. in 22 vols., Grand Rapids: Baker, 1979.

Institutes — *Institutes of the Christian Religion.* Ed. John T. McNeill. Trans. Ford Lewis Battles. 2 vols. Library of Christian Classics, nos. 20–21. Philadelphia: Westminster Press, 1960.

Sermon on Acts — *Sermons on the Acts of the Apostles, Chapters 1–7.* Trans. Rob Roy McGregor. Edinburgh: Banner of Truth Trust, 2008.

Sermon on Deuteronomy — *Sermons on Deuteronomy.* Trans. Arthur Golding. London, 1583. Facsimile reprint ed., Edinburgh: Banner of Truth Trust, 1987.

Sermon on Ephesians — *Sermons on the Epistle to the Ephesians.* Trans. Arthur Golding. Reprint ed., Edinburgh: Banner of Truth Trust, 1973.

Sermon on Galatians — *Sermons on Galatians.* Trans. Kathy Childress. Edinburgh: Banner of Truth Trust, 1997.

Sermon on Timothy or Titus — *Sermons on the Epistles to Timothy & Titus.* Trans. L. T. London: for G. Bishop and T. Woodcoke, 1579. Facsimile reprint ed., Edinburgh: Banner of Truth Trust, 1983.

The selections of Calvin's writings are here presented in semi-purist form. Only small changes have been made, such as the capitalization and lower casing of a few words, the deletion of unnecessary commas and the updating of punctuation, the changing of numerous usages of "upon" to "on" and "which" to "that," the use of contemporary American spelling throughout, and the use of parentheses rather than brackets for the citation of texts. The McNeill-Battles textual citations in the *Institutes* have been retained for the sake of consistency, though some of them are not original to Calvin. On a few occasions, lengthy paragraphs have been broken up into smaller paragraphs for the sake of readability. On rare occasions, a few words have been added in brackets to supply clarity. For the rest, the selections are consistent with what is found in the sources listed above.

The pattern I determined to use in developing selections that represent a cross-section of Calvin's piety is quite simple: to choose three portions of Calvin's writings for every section of the introductory chapter on Calvin's piety. I owe a large debt to Pauline Timmer for selecting and typing up most of the Calvin portions in this volume within these designated parameters. Thanks, too, to Ann Dykema for typing up several of the remaining portions. I am also grateful to Michael Haykin for reading through this manuscript and providing encouragement. And thanks to Martha Fisher and Kristin Meschke for proofreading, to Jay Collier for hunting down the illustrations and seeing this book through the press, to Amy Zevenbergen for working on the cover and illustrations, and to Gary and Linda den Hollander, my effective proofing/typesetting team, for doing their normal high-quality work.

Most of all, I owe heartfelt thanks to my special wife, Mary, for her patience and love in supporting my writing ministry. No man could have a better helpmeet than the one with whom God has graciously chosen to bless me; daily, I thank the Lord and her for such a gift. I also wish to thank my children, Calvin, Esther, and Lydia. Without their great attitude and cooperation, I could never be involved in writing and editing. I want to dedicate this book to my daughter, Esther, who turned a sweet sixteen while this book was being finalized.

Finally, I am so grateful for John Calvin. Much of my life in 2008 has been dedicated to studying him afresh with deep appreciation, and much of 2009 will be dedicated to speaking about his biblical, profound, and experiential teachings at various conferences. What a gift the church has in Calvin! I know of no one who has been more unjustly maligned in church history and no one who could so help the twenty-first century church more than Calvin. Let this little book whet your appetite for reading Calvin's *Institutes*, commentaries, sermons, letters, and treatises. You won't be sorry.

New Year's Day, 2009   Joel R. Beeke

"As soon as he [Peter] has made mention of life he immediately adds godliness [or piety, *pietas*] as if it were *the soul of life*" (emphasis added).

—John Calvin, commenting on 2 Peter 1:3

The 2009 John Calvin 500th Anniversary Commemo-
rative Medal, designed and commissioned by the H.
Henry Meeter Center for Calvin Studies, Hekman
Library, Calvin College. The portrait on the front shows
John Calvin and the heart in the hand image on the
reverse side dates from the mid-16th century.

The Life of John Calvin
(1509–1564)

John Calvin (Jean Cauvin) was so self-effacing that he only wrote about himself three times in his works: in *Reply to Sadoleto* (1539); in the preface to his *Commentary on the Psalms* (1557); and on his deathbed to fellow ministers of Geneva (April 28, 1564), which was recorded by Jean Pinant. After Calvin's death on May 27, 1564, friends discovered that Calvin had given orders to be buried without a tombstone.[1] Four days after his death, the *Geneva Register* simply wrote: "Calvin est allé à Dieu le 27 mai de la presente année." ("Calvin went to God May 27 of the present year.") Shaping this longing for obscurity was Calvin's sincere desire that only God be glorified. In examining Calvin's life and ministry, may we remain true to this driving motif of Calvin's to promote only God.

Early Years[2]

Calvin was born on July 10, 1509, in Noyon, Picardy,

---

1. G. R. Potter and M. Greengrass, *John Calvin* (New York: St. Martin's Press, 1983), 171.

2. For most of this sub-section and the next, I am indebted to my good friend and co-editor of this series, Michael Haykin. The bulk of this chapter is reprinted here with permission from *365 Days with Calvin,* ed. Joel R. Beeke (Leominster, U.K.: Day One, and Grand Rapids: Reformation Heritage Books, 2008).

in northeastern France. The inhabitants of Noyon celebrated in 1551 when a rumor reached their ears that Calvin had died. The following year, after Noyon was destroyed by the Germans, Calvin wrote that he had outlived Noyon. Remarkably, his parents' house was the only structure that remained standing, which Calvin viewed as a miracle.[3]

Calvin's parents were Gérard (d. 1531) and Jeanne Cauvin (d. 1515). Theodore Beza (1519–1605), Calvin's earliest biographer, describes Calvin's parents as "widely respected and in comfortable circumstances."[4] Calvin's father expected Calvin to study for the priesthood. So, in 1520 or 1521, young Calvin was sent to Paris to prepare for the priesthood.

About five years later, Calvin's father sent his son to Orléans to study law for at least two reasons. First, having become a successful lawyer himself, Gérard realized that more money could be made in law than in the priesthood; second, he had become upset with the church when the clergy accused him of wrongfully handling the estate of two priests, which ultimately led to his excommunication from the church in 1528. This sudden, dramatic change of professions for young Calvin is noteworthy also for two reasons. First, Calvin's legal training fostered in him qualities of mind—clarity, precision, and caution—that later served him well as a Bible commentator and theologian. Second, the University of Orléans was where

---

3. Herman J. Selderhuis, *John Calvin: A Pilgrim's Life* (Downers Grove, Ill.: IVP Academic, 2009), 9.

4. Theodore Beza, "The Life of John Calvin," in *The Banner of Truth*, no. 227–228 (August/September 1982), 11.

Calvin first came into contact with Reformation truth. One of his tutors was Melchior Wolmar (1497–1560), an evangelical, who began teaching Greek to Calvin and may well have shared his faith with Calvin. Learning Greek was an important step, for it would open greater riches of the New Testament for Calvin.

Conversion

The date of Calvin's conversion is widely disputed among Reformation scholars. Most scholars cite it as 1533 or early 1534. T. H. L. Parker, however, argues for an earlier date, 1529–1530,[5] as do several recent scholars, including James I. Packer. Though we prefer the traditional date, more important for our purposes is Calvin's account of his conversion. This is what he writes in his preface to his *Commentary on the Psalms* (1557):

> To this pursuit [of the study of law] I endeavored faithfully to apply myself, in obedience to the will of my father; but God, by the secret guidance of his providence, at length gave a different direction to my course. At first, since I was too obstinately devoted to the superstitions of popery to be easily extricated from so profound an abyss of mire, God by a sudden conversion subdued and brought my mind to a teachable frame, which was more hardened in such matters than might have been expected from one at my early period of life. Having thus received some taste and knowledge of true godliness, I was immediately inflamed

5. T. H. L. Parker, *John Calvin: A Biography* (Philadelphia: Westminster Press, 1975), 22, 162–165.

with so intense a desire to make progress therein, that although I did not altogether leave off other studies, I yet pursued them with less ardor.[6]

Five important aspects of this brief, yet longest, account in Calvin's own writing about his conversion should be noted: First, prior to his conversion Calvin says he was "obstinately devoted to the superstitions of popery." He likens himself to a man sunk in a bog, for whom rescue is possible only by an outside hand. Calvin was introduced to papal superstition at an early age. His mother took her son on pilgrimages to shrines and altars to see relics and pray to God and the saints.[7] Calvin felt so stuck in this bog of superstition that only God could deliver him.

Second, Calvin ascribes his rescue to God alone. He mentions no humans used by God to bring him to saving faith. He says nothing of Wolmar; or his cousin, Pierre Olivétain (1506–1538), who translated the New Testament into French; or the early Protestant martyr Étienne de la Forge, with whom Calvin lodged in Paris.[8] Nor does he mention influential works written by Reformers such as Martin Luther (1483–1546). This emphasis on the absolute sovereignty of God in salvation, however, was typical of Calvin and the Reformers.

Third, Calvin says his conversion was "sudden," taken from the Latin *subita*, which can mean "unex-

---

6. *Commentary on The Book of Psalms*, trans. James Anderson (repr., Grand Rapids: Baker Book House, 1979), 1:xl–xli.

7. Ronald S. Wallace, *Calvin, Geneva and the Reformation* (Grand Rapids: Baker Book House, 1988), 2.

8. Ibid., 7.

John Calvin and his cousin in friendly controversy.

pected." Calvin's conversion was not the result of his own wish or intent.[9] Indeed, Calvin was known to be resistant to change. But God broke into his life, causing a dramatic upheaval that changed his view of God and led him to embrace evangelical doctrine.

Fourth, God overcame Calvin's natural stubbornness, which gave way to gospel peace. As Calvin says, God "subdued and brought my mind to a teachable frame." In that teachable frame, Calvin experienced that conversion meant freedom from the bondage of Rome and liberation from the torments of conscience. As the Spirit taught him that salvation is in Christ alone, Calvin experienced unspeakable peace, saying, "There is no greater good one can inherit on this earth."[10]

Fifth, Calvin was so "inspired by a taste of true religion" that he lost interest in studying the law. Out of respect for his father, he did not immediately drop out of the law program, but that study became less critical than his primary goal to progress in true piety and godliness.

Some scholars depict Calvin as cold and unemotional. But this account of his conversion reveals an unusually ardent nature. As James A. de Jong has said, all one has to do is examine Calvin's prayers to find "an experiential believer of considerable... warmth."[11]

---

9. Parker, *John Calvin,* 163.

10. Selderhuis, *John Calvin: A Pilgrim's Life,* 21.

11. Cited in J. Nigel Westhead, "Calvin and Experimental Knowledge of God," in *Adorning the Doctrine. Papers read at the 1995 Westminster Conference* (London: The Westminster Conference, 1995), 16.

Calvin's conversion was nothing less than an unreserved, wholehearted commitment to the living God. For the rest of his life, Calvin would pledge allegiance to God. As Herman Selderhuis says, "Calvin became God's advocate. He would devote every minute of the rest of his life to the defense of God and of his cause."[12] This ardent commitment is evident in his crest, or seal, which shows a heart upon an open hand, with the motto underneath: "My heart I give Thee, Lord, eagerly and earnestly"—or, as it could also be translated, willingly and honestly—traits that no one can deny accurately describe Calvin's entire life. The seal was also bookended with the letters *I* and *C*—did they stand for *Ioannes Calvinus*, or for *Iesus Christus*, or both? In any case, "it was Calvin's desire that all that concerned him and all that concerned Christ should be perfectly aligned, but should also actually come together as one."[13]

Calvin Comes to Geneva

In less than a year, people began to flock to Calvin to be taught pure doctrine. Teaching the evangelical faith was dangerous in France, and Calvin was soon forced to flee because of persecution. He went to Basel in January 1535, where the elderly Erasmus (1466/1469–1536); Heinrich Bullinger (1504–1575), friend and successor of Huldreich Zwingli (1484–1531) at Zurich; Guillaume Farel (1489–1565); and Pierre Olivétain were staying. While there, Calvin began working on *Institutes of the Christian Religion,*

---

12. Selderhuis, *John Calvin: A Pilgrim's Life,* 22.
13. Ibid., 29.

which would later become a classic work of Reformed theology.

After a year or so at Basel, Calvin went to Italy. He settled in Ferrara, where he hoped to work as secretary to Princess Renée, sister-in-law of Francis I, King of France. Calvin wanted to live there permanently as an obscure scholar, but that did not work out so he returned to France. He only stayed there six months because he could not agree with the conditions of the Edict of Lyons (May 31, 1536), which "allowed heretics to live in the kingdom on the condition that they were reconciled to Rome within six months."[14]

Calvin planned to go to Strasbourg to gain some support from Martin Bucer (1491–1551), the German Reformer, and carve out for himself the quiet life of a scholar in "some obscure corner," but the main road was closed. So he took a different route by way of Geneva, intending to stay one night there.

Not long before Calvin's arrival, Geneva (pop. 10,000–15,000) had declared itself pro-Reformation, largely due to the fiery preaching of Guillaume Farel, an indefatigable evangelist, and Pierre Viret (1511–1571). Calvin describes the condition of Geneva in his preface to his *Commentary on the Psalms*: "Popery had been driven from (Geneva) by the exertions of… (Guillaume Farel), and Peter Viret; but matters were not yet brought to a settled state, and the city was divided into unholy and dangerous factions."[15]

Farel discovered that Calvin was staying in the city and went to see him. He knew of Calvin from reading

---

14. Parker, *John Calvin*, 52.

15. *Commentary on The Book of Psalms*, 1:xlii.

the first edition of the *Institutes* (1536).[16] He discerned that Calvin was just the sort of man to assist him in Geneva, especially since Farel was more of a pioneer and evangelist than pastor and teacher. He asked Calvin to stay in Geneva and help him. Calvin was adamant about going to Strasbourg. Farel persisted, threatening that Calvin's lot would be like Jonah's if he abandoned the Nineveh of Geneva. Calvin later wrote, "Finding that he gained nothing by entreaties, (Farel) proceeded to utter an imprecation that God would curse my retirement, and the tranquility of the studies which I sought, if I should withdraw and refuse to give assistance." Calvin was stricken with terror, feeling "as if God had from heaven laid his mighty hand upon me to arrest me."[17] So Calvin stayed in Geneva.

Calvin's commentary on Matthew 8:19 captures the essence of his encounter with Farel. Matthew tells about a scribe who comes to our Lord Jesus and tells

---

16. Remarkably, Calvin wrote the *Institutes* at the age of twenty-six, only a few years after his conversion. The first edition consisted of six chapters that covered the law (the Ten Commandments), a summary of faith (Apostles' Creed), prayer (the Lord's Prayer), the sacraments, and Christian liberty and responsibility. It was immediately hailed by Protestants as a major achievement in producing an apology for and an introductory overview to the Protestant faith. The first edition was not even fifteen percent of the size of the final edition that would appear in 1559, five years before Calvin died. Calvin continued to work for most of his life expanding and refining his theological classic, which he rightly understood to be his most important book. Cf. François Wendel, *Calvin: Origins and Development of His Religious Thought,* trans. Philip Mairet (Grand Rapids: Baker, 2002), 111–149.

17. Preface to the *Commentary on the Psalms*, 1:xlii.

Him that he would follow Him wherever He would go. Calvin writes:

> We must bear in mind that he was a scribe who had been accustomed to a quiet and easy life, had enjoyed honor, and was ill-fitted to endure reproaches, poverty, persecutions, and the cross. He wishes indeed to follow Christ but dreams of an easy and agreeable life and of dwellings filled with every convenience, whereas the disciples of Christ must walk among thorns and march to the cross amidst uninterrupted afflictions. The more eager he is, the less he is prepared. He seems as if he wished to fight in the shade and at ease, annoyed neither by sweat nor by dust, and beyond the reach of the weapons of war.... Let us therefore look upon ourselves as warned, in his person, not to boast lightly and at ease that we will be the disciples of Christ, while we are taking no thought of the cross or of afflictions; but, on the contrary, to consider early what sort of condition awaits us. The first lesson which he [i.e., Christ] gives us, on entering his school, is *to deny ourselves, and take up his cross* (Matt. 16:24).[18]

Calvin's First Ministry in Geneva (1536–1538)

Calvin almost immediately began to serve as lecturer, commencing with exegeting the epistles of Paul, and was soon called to pastor in Geneva as well, both of which met with considerable success. Nevertheless, throughout his first ministry in Geneva, Calvin was

---

18. *Commentary on a Harmony of the Evangelists, Matthew, Mark, and Luke*, trans. William Pringle (repr., Grand Rapids: Baker Book House, 1979), 1:388.

plagued by dissensions in the city, especially by some Anabaptists. He also had rather tense relations with the city council. Early on, Calvin concluded that if Geneva was to become thoroughly Reformed, the church needed a confession to which all citizens in Geneva should subscribe. Then, too, a pattern of discipline should be introduced so that everyone would not only formally embrace the Protestant faith but would become more disciplined under the Word of God. Calvin believed the church needed the authority

Interior of the Cathedral of Geneva

to excommunicate immoral people so that the purity of the church might be maintained.

The city council was prepared to have a common confession of faith but was not so willing to vest the power of excommunication in the preachers. They feared that such great power could lead to civil unrest; besides, who knows what unstable preachers might do? They might even excommunicate a city councilman! So the council insisted that the ultimate authority of excommunication should remain under its own control.

This tension between the church and the government was exacerbated when Calvin and his fellow preachers in Geneva tried to foster a more disciplined life in the city. Many Genevans resented this intrusion from foreign or "outside preachers." Eventually, Calvin's theology, ethics, and ecclesiastical vision were complicated by the politics of the day. By 1538, some of Calvin's opponents who wanted to keep strong political ties with Bern at all costs—even if it meant banishing Calvin—had been elected to the city council. As foreigners, Calvin and Farel were now easy targets; when they insisted that certain people needed to be excommunicated before Easter 1538, the city council reneged. When the Reformers then refused to administer the Lord's Supper at all, the city council exiled Calvin and Farel from Geneva for insubordination. That was less than two years after Calvin's arrival.

Calvin received the expulsion with mixed emotions. "Geneva is bound on my heart so fully, I would have gladly given my life for its welfare," he wrote. At the same time, he said, "My Master's will be done. If we had served men, we would have been ill rewarded, but we serve a good Master who will reward us, even in expulsion."[19] For Calvin, the fear of God prevailed over the fear of man; so long as he retained divine approval, he was content to be a laughingstock and object of ridicule.

Calvin in Strasbourg (1538–1541)

Calvin wanted to go to Basel, but he heeded Martin Bucer's pressing invitation to take leadership of the French-speaking Protestant refugee congregation of nearly five hundred people in Strasbourg. Calvin lived in Strasbourg for three years—some of the happiest years of his life. Not only could he freely follow his long-cherished desire of pursuing his scholarly career in Strasbourg, but his experience there, under the influence of Bucer, influenced him in a number of ways.

First, Bucer inspired Calvin to be a biblical commentator. Though Calvin viewed Bucer as a mentor of keen insight and learning, he felt that Bucer's biblical expositions were long-winded. Bucer influenced Calvin to begin his career as a great biblical commentator in Strasbourg, which was something in which Calvin would far excel his mentor.

Second, Calvin was impressed by the church order that Bucer established in Strasbourg. Bucer promoted four offices: doctor/teacher, pastor, elder, and deacon. Calvin later implemented this structure in Geneva as the model he regarded as most biblical.

---

19. Cited in John T. McNeill, *The History and Character of Calvinism* (Oxford: Oxford University Press, 1954), 143.

Third, Calvin was impressed with the order of worship that Bucer introduced into the life of the Strasbourg church. While in Strasbourg, Calvin created an order for worship according to the local practice. His later order of worship in Geneva leaned heavily on this work.

Fourth, Calvin was impressed by the school system that Bucer and his educational leader, Johann Sturm (1507–1589), established in Strasbourg. Calvin taught in Sturm's new academy, which later served as a model for Calvin's own Geneva Academy for the training of ministers and young people.

Finally, Calvin was impressed with a young Anabaptist widow in Strasbourg, Idelette de Bure (ca. 1499–1549), whom he later married. Calvin was so impressed with Idelette that he once said he would rather travel to eternity in her shoes than in anyone else's in the world. Calvin's nine years of marriage with Idelette, however, were not unclouded ones. Calvin's letters are full of references to Idelette's various illnesses throughout their short marriage. The one child given to them, Jacques, born on July 28, 1542, died only twenty-two days after his birth. The Roman Catholics viewed Calvin's inability to have children as an act of God's judgment against him, but Calvin's response was that he had myriads of spiritual children all over the world of whom Rome was utterly unaware. Though Calvin inherited Idelette's two children, a son and a daughter, by a previous marriage and became their only surviving parent after her death, treating them as his own children as he had promised Idelette, nothing could replace his loyal partner. Idelette's death on March

Cardinal Sadoleto's visit to Calvin

29, 1549, was a heavy blow. Calvin said he had lost his best friend; he wrote to a friend, "I am no more than half a man, since God recently took my wife home to himself.... I am forced to go on, but I hardly have courage to do so."[20]

Calvin's Second Ministry in Geneva (1541–1564)

By 1541, Roman Catholics appeared to be making headway in nudging Geneva back to Catholicism. Cardinal Jacopo Sadoleto (1477–1547), the reforming bishop of Carpentras, had written a public letter to the Genevans, pleading with them to return to the holy mother church. The Genevan city council asked Calvin to respond, which he did most effectively in his *Reply to Sadoleto,* one of the best early summaries of the

---

20. McNeill, *History and Character of Calvinism*, 156–157.

Reformed church's doctrinal position. Recognizing the need for strong, Protestant leadership, the city council invited Calvin to return to Geneva. After reluctantly agreeing to do so, Calvin promptly threw himself into the hard work of reforming Geneva. That task would consume the last twenty-four years of his life. Calvin's second ministry in Geneva can be divided into two parts: years of opposition and years of support.

Years of Opposition (1541–1555)

In Geneva, one of Calvin's first responsibilities was to write various laws for the new republic. He drafted a new order of worship, a new catechism, and a new church ordinance, all of which, with various amendments, were eventually approved by the city council. Calvin offered a church and society structure that would cultivate the sharing of power between the church and the state as two separate kingdoms. Calvin's structure, which was greatly influenced by Bucer, would resonate in varying degrees throughout the European continent.

Calvin's *Ecclesiastical Ordinances,* which clearly defined the order of congregational life, gave the Reformed church autonomy in matters of faith and morals. The church was to exercise its power through four orders of ministry: pastors, doctors (i.e., teachers or lecturers), elders, and deacons.[21] The pastors were to preach frequently, to engage fervently in intercessory prayer, to administer the sacraments faithfully, and to shepherd the congregation conscien-

---

21. David F. Wright, "Calvin's Role in Church History," in *The Cambridge Companion to John Calvin,* ed. Donald K. McKim (Cambridge: Cambridge University Press, 2004), 284.

tiously. The doctors were to focus on the theological training of seminarians and pastors, provide regular theological lectures, instruct the young, and guard the church's doctrinal purity. The elders, who were laymen, were responsible for assisting the pastors in maintaining supervision and discipline over the lives of members. They were also to engage in consistent intercessory prayer. The deacons were divided into two orders—the first to manage the church's resources and give administrative oversight; the second, to visit the sick and needy and lead the church in the ministry of mercy and charity.

The pastors and doctors formed a group called the Venerable Company, which met weekly for Bible study. Calvin moderated the Venerable Company and presented its recommendations to the city councils. The pastors and elders met in a body called the consistory once a week to provide pastoral counsel, censure conduct, and draw in new members. The deacons also met weekly to carry out their tasks.[22]

Alongside this church structure, the city formed a pyramid of three councils that included the smallest and most powerful council of twenty-four (usually called the city council) and the larger, less powerful city councils of sixty and one hundred. Neither the ecclesiastic nor the civic side of Geneva fully achieved its goals but managed to work together despite unresolved tension for many years. For example, all the city councils had some say in choosing the church's

---

22. Derek Thomas, "Reforming the Church," in Joel R. Beeke, *Living for God's Glory: An Introduction to Calvinism* (Lake Mary, Fla.: Reformation Trust, 2008), 225–227.

elders, but the pastors themselves were allowed to choose the pastors.

The rumor that Calvin was a tyrant in Geneva and ruled with an iron hand is patently false. Calvin never held a civic office in Geneva. He was not even a citizen of the city until well into the 1550s. His position was not secure in Geneva until 1555, when his enemies (the Libertines) failed to be reelected to the city council.

Whatever influence Calvin had in Geneva during the 1540s and the first half of the 1550s was based on the moral authority of his preaching, teaching, and wisdom. Even then, the city council often operated against his judgment and recommendations. For example, Calvin wanted weekly communion, but the city council insisted that communion should be administered only four times a year. Then, too, Calvin faced major battles with various individuals, including the Reformed humanist Sebastian Castellio (1513–1563), the council-leader Ami Perrin, the free-thinker Jacques Gruet, the ex-Carmelite Jerome Bolsec (d. 1584), the rambunctious Philibert Berthelier, and the antitrinitarian Michael Servetus (ca. 1511–1553). Prolonged battles with each of these men took a heavy toll on Calvin in the midst of these busy years.

Despite formidable opposition, Calvin maintained an intense preaching schedule. Until 1549, Calvin preached twice on Sunday, at one of the two morning services, then again in the afternoon. He also spoke three times during the week.[23] In October 1549, the

---

23. T. H. L. Parker, *The Oracles of God. An Introduction to the Preaching of John Calvin* (London: Lutterworth Press, 1947), 33.

number of sermons increased from once every other day to once a day by order of the city council.[24]

Calvin's frequent, faithful preaching bore fruit in the conversion of individual Genevans. In due time, the city councils also swung Calvin's way.

Years of support (1555–1564)
When the Libertines were defeated in 1555, the city council finally became supportive of Calvin and conceded the long-disputed right of excommunication to the consistory. Geneva became Calvin's city at last! For the last nine years of his life, Calvin implemented many of his long-cherished visions. In his final decade, more than any other, Calvin revealed his skill as an able teacher of theology, a biblical writer, a faithful preacher, a wise counselor, and a seasoned church leader.

In 1558, Calvin established the Geneva Academy, which was divided into a "private school" (*schola privata*) for elementary instruction and a "public school" (*schola publica*), which offered more advanced studies in biblical languages and theology. Calvin's friend and successor, Theodore Beza, served as the first rector of the school. Students came to the academy from all over the world. When Calvin died, the school had 1,200 junior and 300 senior students. Men trained for the ministry fanned out from Geneva into many other countries in Europe. Most went to France, where the Reformed movement grew to about ten percent of the population prior to the St. Bartholomew's Day massacre. A significant number of pastors and lay leaders

24. Ibid., 39.

The Geneva Academy

also went to Britain (e.g., John Knox, the reformer of Scotland), Germany (e.g., Caspar Olevianus, the reformer of the Palatinate), and the Netherlands (e.g., the Marnix brothers, lay leaders of the Reformed movement there). In those countries, Calvin's followers—often with his assistance—adopted various confessional statements to strengthen the Reformed cause. Eventually, the academy evolved into the University of Geneva.

In 1559, Calvin completed his final, definitive edition of the *Institutes,* which became the most famous book of Reformed theology ever written. Following the overall structure of the Apostles' Creed, Calvin divided this work into four books. The first book is on God the Creator, and on man, brought into creation by God. This book discusses the providence of God and the oversight of God over all things. The second book covers the fall of man into sin, the character of sin, and the work of Christ in redeeming man from sin. The third book explains how the Holy Spirit applies redemption to mankind. The fourth book is primarily on the church—the character of the church from a positive point of view, the negative deformation of the church in the Middle Ages, and, finally, the proper relationship of church and state.

Calvin wrote many more works in his last decade, including commentaries, sermons, and treatises on a great variety of subjects. He also wrote voluminous letters from his study and his sickbed encouraging and instructing pastors and persecuted believers throughout Europe to persevere in the doctrines of grace. He was a spiritual and practical counselor to thousands. To his fellow ministers gathered around his deathbed, Calvin said, "God has given me grace to write what I have written as faithfully as it was in my power. I have not falsified a single passage of the Scriptures, nor given it a wrong interpretation to the best of my knowledge."[25]

Counting his posthumous works, Calvin's collected writings fill fifty-nine large folio volumes in the *Corpus Reformatorum* (a 101-volume set of important Reformation works) and twelve volumes of *Supplementa Calviniana*.[26] This includes commentaries on twenty-four of the thirty-nine Old Testament books

---

25. Cited in Parker, *John Calvin,* 154.

26. Karl Gottlieb Bretschneider, et al., eds, *Corpus Reformatorum,* 101 vols. (Halle: Schwetske, 1863–1900). Hereafter, *CO.* The Calvin works compose Series 2 of this collection, *Ioannis Calvini, Opera Quae Supersunt Omnia,* vols. 29–87. Hereafter, *CO.* Cf. Robert Reymond,

and twenty-four of the twenty-seven New Testament books (all except 2 and 3 John and Revelation). The biblical fidelity, practicality, and experiential depth of Calvin's writings are unsurpassed in Protestant history.

To the end of his life, however, Calvin viewed his most important work in Geneva as "proclaiming the Word of God" and "instructing believers in wholesome doctrine." Though he was heavily involved in pastoring pastors and people, the center of his ministry was preaching the gospel. In 1561, Beza claimed in a letter to Farel that over a thousand people heard Calvin preach on a daily basis.[27] Calvin himself repeatedly said that it is through preaching that God reveals Himself in judgment and mercy, turning hearts to obedience, confirming the faith of believers, and building up and purifying the church.

Calvin delivered his sermons from memory without prepared texts. His method of preaching was like that of Zwingli and some church fathers, such as John Chrysostom (ca. 347–407). He did not choose a single text or isolated passage. Rather, he preached steadily through book after book of the Bible, often taking the better part of a year to complete a Bible book. On Sundays, he concentrated on the New Testament, except for a few Psalms on Sunday afternoons, interrupting his method only on special feast days such as Christmas and Easter. During the week, he

John Calvin: His Life and Influence (Ross-shire, U.K.: Christian Focus, 2004), 13n.

27. David W. Hall, *The Legacy of John Calvin: His Influence on the Modern World* (Phillipsburg, N.J.: P & R, 2008), 60.

preached through the Old Testament, book by book.[28] T. H. L. Parker notes: "Those in Geneva who listened Sunday after Sunday, day after day, and did not shut their ears…received a training in Christianity such as had been given to few congregations in Europe since the days of the fathers."[29] And in the words of Steve Lawson: "Calvin's preaching was biblical in its substance, sequential in its pattern, direct in its message, extemporaneous in its delivery, exegetical in its approach, accessible in its simplicity, pastoral in its tone, polemic in its defense of the truth, passionate in its outreach, and doxological in its conclusion."[30] It was also practical and experiential in its emphases.

Calvin's last years were packed with evangelistic endeavors, particularly in France, but also as far away as Brazil. Geneva-trained ministers and missionaries also planted churches in the Netherlands, Italy, Poland, Germany, Hungary, England, and Scotland. Everywhere Calvin's advice was sought and gladly given.[31]

Calvin's Death and Influence

Calvin's health could not keep pace with his incredible workload. During the last years of his life, he battled numerous diseases. Doctors, fellow Reform-

---

28. T. H. L. Parker, *Portrait of Calvin* (London: SCM Press, 1954), 82.

29. Parker, *John Calvin,* 92.

30. Steven J. Lawson, "The Preacher of God's Word," in *John Calvin: A Heart for Devotion, Doctrine, and Doxology,* ed. Burk Parsons (Lake Mary, Fla.: Reformation Trust, 2008), 72–79.

31. Joel R. Beeke, "Calvin's Evangelism," *Puritan Reformed Spirituality* (Darlington, U.K.: Evangelical Press, 2004), chap. 3.

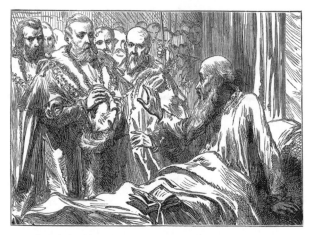

Calvin addressing the council for the last time

ers, students, and friends advised him to stop working, but his answer was: "What! Would my Lord find me idle?"[32]

On February 2, 1564, Calvin gave his last lecture on a passage from Ezekiel, and being carried to the pulpit on a bed, he preached his last sermon the following Sunday. On April 2, he attended church and took part in the Lord's Supper for the last time. Late that month, he invited the Little Council (April 27) and the consistory of Geneva (April 28) around his deathbed, where he gave them a final testimony, had a final discussion, and asked for forgiveness for his shortcomings. His testimony was clear until his

---

32. Theodore Beza, *The Life of John Calvin* in *The Banner of Truth*, no. 227–228: 56–57.

final day, May 27, 1564, when his soul passed into glory at the age of fifty-five. The following day, he was granted his wish to be buried in a plain wooden coffin in an unmarked grave in the cemetery of Plein Palais, so that human glory would not rob God of the exclusive glory that He deserves.

Soli Deo Gloria (the glory of God alone) is what Calvin's life and theology are all about. This is the common theme of Calvin the theologian, Calvin the reformer, Calvin the pastor-counselor, Calvin the churchman, Calvin the evangelist, and Calvin the writer. In every area of his personal life and ministry, Calvin was wholeheartedly committed to God and His glory, and he yearned only to promote the pre-eminence of Christ in dependency on the Spirit.

Primarily through his writings, Calvin's influence has lived on through the centuries and permeated millions of hearts. Today that influence is commonly called Calvinism and is nearly synonymous with the Reformed faith. The threefold influence of Calvin's Calvinism has been summarized by Burk Parsons as "devotion, doctrine, and doxology—the heart's devotion to the biblical God, the mind's pursuit of the biblical doctrine of God, and the entire being's surrender to doxology."[33]

Calvinism's greatest influence was in Britain and its North American colonies, the Netherlands, Hungary, and parts of Germany. In all of these areas, and many more around the world—including Poland, Italy, Brazil, South Africa, Malawi, Zambia, Austra-

---

33. Parsons, *John Calvin: A Heart for Devotion, Doctrine, and Doxology,* 5.

lia, New Zealand, Singapore, South Korea, China, the Philippines, Russia, Egypt, Pakistan, India, and Israel—Calvinism is still being propagated today. Truly, Calvinism has a bright future, for it offers much to people who seek to believe and practice the whole counsel of God. Calvinism aims to do so with both clear-headed faith and warm-hearted piety, producing vibrant living in the home, the church, and the marketplace to the glory of God.

Today, Calvin's legacy is extended to us in additional ways. David Hall suggests ten key ways that our culture is different because of Calvin. He includes education, care for the poor, ethics, church autonomy, collegial governing, decentralized politics, parity among professions, economics, the Psalter, and printing books.[34]

This book aims to capture some of Calvin's authentic, devotional piety and doxology that promote God's whole counsel. Cotton Mather writes that John Cotton, on being asked why in his later days he indulged in nightly studies, pleasantly replied, "Because I love to sweeten my mouth with a piece of Calvin before I go to sleep."[35] It is our prayer that this spirit of genuine piety that so enveloped Calvin and Cotton may also penetrate you as you read this book.

---

34. Hall, *Legacy of John Calvin,* 13–41.

35. Cotton Mather, *The Great Works of Christ in America* (Edinburgh: Banner of Truth Trust, 1979), 1:274.

The Piety of John Calvin

Few people enjoy being called pietistic today. Tragically, *piety* and its English derivatives have become pejorative words and concepts. John Calvin would be aghast. For him, piety was not only a positive trait, it was the essence of true biblical Christianity. For Calvin, the preeminent systematician of the Protestant Reformation, theological understanding and practical piety, truth and usefulness, were inseparable. Theology deals first with knowledge—knowledge of God and of ourselves—but there is no true knowledge where there is no true piety.

Calvin's concept of piety (*pietas*) was rooted in the knowledge of God and included attitudes and actions that were directed to the adoration and service of God.[1] Piety is one of the major themes of Calvin's theology. John T. McNeill says that Calvin's theology is "piety described at length."[2] Indeed, Calvin was determined to confine theology within the limits of piety.[3] In the

1. Serene Jones, *Calvin and the Rhetoric of Piety* (Louisville: Westminster /John Knox, 1995).

2. Quoted in John Hesselink, "The Development and Purpose of Calvin's Institutes," in *Articles on Calvin and Calvinism, Vol. 4: Influences upon Calvin and Discussion of the 1559 Institutes*, ed. Richard C. Gamble (New York: Garland, 1992), 215–216.

3. See Brian A. Gerrish, "Theology within the Limits of Piety Alone: Schleiermacher and Calvin's Doctrine of God" (1981),

preface to his *Institutes*, which was addressed to King Francis I, Calvin says that the book's purpose is "solely to transmit certain rudiments by which those who are touched with any zeal for religion might be shaped to true godliness [*pietas*]."[4] This comprehensive sense of piety profoundly impacted Calvin's successors (such as the English Puritans, Dutch Further Reformation divines, and some of the German Pietists and their descendants) down to the present day.

After an introductory look at the definition and purpose of piety in Calvin's thinking, this chapter will show how Calvin's piety impacted the theological, ecclesiological, and practical dimensions of his thought.[5]

The Definition and Importance of Piety

For Calvin, piety designates a proper attitude toward God and obedience to Him. Flowing out of the knowledge of who and what God is (theology), piety includes heartfelt worship, saving faith, filial fear, prayerful submission, and reverential love.[6]

---

reprinted in *The Old Protestantism and the New: Essays on the Reformation Heritage* (Chicago: University of Chicago Press, 1982), chap. 12.

4. John Calvin, *Institutes of the Christian Religion,* ed. John T. McNeill, trans. Ford Lewis Battles (Philadelphia: Westminster Press, 1960), 9.

5. Most of this chapter is abridged from Joel R. Beeke, "Calvin on Piety," in *The Cambridge Companion to John Calvin,* ed. Donald K. McKim (Cambridge: Cambridge University Press, 2004), 125–152.

6. Cf. Lucien Joseph Richard, *The Spirituality of John Calvin* (Atlanta: John Knox Press, 1974), 100–101; Sou-Young Lee, "Calvin's Understanding of *Pietas,*" in *Calvinus Sincerioris Religionis Vindex,* ed. W. H. Neuser and B. G. Armstrong (Kirksville, Mo.: Sixteenth Century Studies, 1997), 226–233; and H. W. Simpson, "*Pietas* in the

In his first catechism, Calvin writes, "True piety consists in a sincere feeling which loves God as Father as much as it fears and reverences Him as Lord, embraces His righteousness, and dreads offending Him worse than death."[7] In the *Institutes*, Calvin writes, "I call 'piety' that reverence joined with love of God which the knowledge of his benefits induces."[8] This love and reverence for God is a necessary concomitant to true knowledge of Him.

Such piety embraces all of life. Calvin writes, "The whole life of Christians ought to be a sort of practice of godliness"[9]— or, as the subtitle of the first edition of the *Institutes* states, "Embracing almost the whole sum of piety & whatever is necessary to know of the doctrine of salvation: A work most worthy to be read by all persons zealous for piety."[10]

Institutes of Calvin," in *Reformational Tradition: A Rich Heritage and Lasting Vocation* (Potchefstroom, South Africa: Potchefstroom University for Christian Higher Education, 1984), 179–191.

7. Ed. and trans. Ford Lewis Battles (Pittsburgh: Pittsburgh Theological Seminary), 2.

8. Institutes, 1.2.1.

9. Institutes, 3.19.2.

10. *Institutes of the Christian Religion: 1536 Edition*, trans. Ford Lewis Battles, rev. ed. (Grand Rapids: Eerdmans, 1986). The original Latin title reads: *Christianae religionis institutio total fere pietatis summam et quidquid est in doctrina salutis cognitu necessarium complectens, omnibut pietatis studiosis lectu dignissimum opus ac recens editum* (*Joannis Calvini opera selecta*, ed. Peter Barth, Wilhelm Niesel, and Dora Scheuner, 5 vols. [Munich: Chr. Kaiser, 1926–1952], 1:19). From 1539 on, the titles were simply *Institutio Christianae Religionis*, but "zeal for piety" continued to be a great goal of Calvin's work. See Richard A. Muller, *The Unaccommodated Calvin: Studies in the Foundation of a Theological Tradition* (New York: Oxford University Press, 2000), 106–107.

Piety's Supreme Goal: *Soli Deo Gloria*

The goal of piety is to recognize and praise the glory of God—glory that shines in God's attributes, in the structure of the world, and in the death and resurrection of Jesus Christ.[11] The desire to glorify God supersedes even the desire for personal salvation in every truly pious person.[12] We were created that God might be glorified in us, and the regenerate yearn to live out this purpose.[13] Furthermore, God redeems, adopts, and sanctifies His people that His glory would shine in them and deliver them from impious self-seeking.[14] As a result, the pious man's deepest concern is God Himself and the things of God—God's Word, God's authority, God's gospel, God's truth. He yearns to know more of God and to commune more with Him.

But how do we glorify God? Calvin writes: "God has prescribed for us a way in which he will be glorified by us, namely, piety, which consists in the obedience of his Word. He that exceeds these bounds does not go about to honor God, but rather to dishonor him."[15] Obedience to God's Word means taking refuge in Christ for forgiveness of our sins, knowing Him through the Scriptures, serving Him with a loving heart, doing good works in gratitude for His goodness, and exercising self-denial to the point

---

11. Institutes, 3.2.1; *CO* 43:428, 47:316.

12. *CO* 26:693.

13. *CO* 24:362.

14. *CO* 26:225, 29:5, 51:147.

15. *CO* 49:51.

Young Calvin expounding the Bible
to a family at Bourges

of loving our enemies.[16] This response involves total surrender to God Himself, His Word, and His will (Rom. 11:33–12:2).[17]

Calvin's motto well sums up the piety with which he lived: "I offer thee my heart, Lord, promptly and sincerely." This is the desire of all who are truly pious. However, this desire can be realized only through communion with Christ and participation in Him, for outside of Christ even the most religious person lives for himself. Only in Christ can the pious live as willing servants of their Lord, faithful soldiers of their Commander, and obedient children of their Father.[18]

---

16. *CO* 26:166, 33:186, 47:377–378, 49:245, 51:21.
17. *CO* 6:9–10.
18. *CO* 26:439–440.

Theological Dimensions

There are a number of theological dimensions to this understanding of piety. They include:

• *Piety's profound root: mystical union.* Piety is rooted in the believer's mystical union with Christ, so this union must be our starting point.[19] Such a union is possible because Christ took on our human nature, filling it with His sinless virtue. Union with Christ in His humanity is historical, ethical, and personal. However, we do not lose our identity in Him; there is no thought of a mixture of human substances between Christ and us. Nonetheless, Calvin states, "Not only does he cleave to us by an indivisible bond of fellowship, but with a wonderful communion, day by day, he grows more and more into one body with us, until he becomes completely one with us."[20] This union is one of the gospel's greatest mysteries.[21] Because of Christ's perfection in our nature, the pious may draw by faith whatever they need for their sanctification (John 6:51).[22]

If Christ had died and risen but had not applied His salvation to believers for their regeneration and

---

19. Howard G. Hageman, "Reformed Spirituality," in *Protestant Spiritual Traditions,* ed. Frank C. Senn (New York: Paulist Press, 1986), 61.

20. Institutes, 3.2.24.

21. Dennis Tamburello points out that "at least seven instances occur in the *Institutes* where Calvin uses the word *arcanus* or *incomprehensibilis* to describe union with Christ" (2.12.7; 3.11.5; 4.17.1, 9, 31, 33; 4.19.35; *Union with Christ: John Calvin and the Mysticism of St. Bernard* [Louisville: Westminster /John Knox, 1994], 89, 144).

22. *Commentary* on John 6:51.

sanctification, His work would have been ineffectual. Our piety shows that the Spirit of Christ is working in us what already has been accomplished in Christ. Christ administers His sanctification to the church so that the church may live piously for Him.[23]

• *Piety's double bond: the Spirit and faith.* Union and communion with Christ are realized only through Spirit-worked faith, Calvin teaches. Communion is actual, not because believers participate in the essence of Christ's nature, but because the Spirit of Christ unites believers so intimately to Christ that they become, as it were, flesh of His flesh and bone of His bone. From God's perspective, the Spirit is the bond between Christ and believers, whereas from our perspective, faith is the bond. These perspectives do not contradict each other, since one of the Spirit's principal operations is to work faith in a sinner.[24]

Only the Spirit can unite Christ in heaven with the believer on earth. Just as the Spirit united heaven and earth in the incarnation, so in regeneration He raises the elect from earth to commune with Christ in heaven and brings Christ into the hearts and lives of the elect on earth.[25] Thus, communion with Christ is always the result of the Spirit's work—a work that is astonishing and experiential rather than comprehensible.[26] The Holy Spirit is the link that binds the

---

23. Institutes, 2.16.16.
24. Institutes, 3.1.4.
25. Institutes, 4.17.6; *Commentary* on Acts 15:9.
26. *Commentary* on Ephesians 5:32.

believer to Christ, the channel through which Christ is communicated to the believer.[27]

Faith unites the believer to Christ by means of the Word, enabling the believer to receive Christ as He is clothed in the gospel and graciously offered by the Father.[28] Consequently, Calvin says, "We ought not to separate Christ from ourselves or ourselves from him," but participate in Christ by faith, for this "revives us from death to make us a new creature."[29]

By faith, the believer possesses Christ and grows in Him. What's more, the degree of his faith exercised through the Word determines his degree of communion with Christ.[30] "Everything which faith should contemplate is exhibited to us in Christ," Calvin writes.[31] The believer who excels in piety learns to grasp Christ so firmly by faith that Christ dwells within his heart, though He remains in heaven.[32] The pious live by what they find in Christ rather than by what they find in themselves.[33]

• *Piety's double cleansing: justification and sanctification.* According to Calvin, believers receive from Christ by faith the "double grace" of justification and sanctifi-

---

27. Institutes, 3.1.1, 4.17.12.

28. Institutes, 3.2.30–32.

29. Institutes, 3.2.24; *Commentary* on 1 John 2:12.

30. John Calvin, *Sermons on the Epistle to the Ephesians*, trans. Arthur Golding (1577; reprint Edinburgh: Banner of Truth Trust, 1973), 1:17–18. Hereafter, *Sermon* on Ephesians text.

31. *Commentary* on Ephesians 3:12.

32. *Sermon* on Ephesians 3:14–19.

33. *Commentary* on Habakkuk 2:4.

cation, which together provide a twofold cleansing.[34] Justification offers imputed purity while sanctification brings actual purity.[35]

Calvin views justification as including the remission of sins and the right to eternal life, by which "God receives us into his favor as righteous men."[36] He goes on to say that "since God justifies us by the intercession of Christ, he absolves us not by the confirmation of our own innocence but by the imputation of righteousness, so that we who are not righteous in ourselves may be reckoned as such in Christ."[37]

Calvin also regards justification as "the principal hinge by which religion is supported," the soil out of which the Christian life develops, and the substance of piety.[38] Justification not only serves God's honor by satisfying the conditions for salvation, it also gives the believer's conscience "peaceful rest and serene tranquility."[39] As Romans 5:1 says, "Therefore being justified by faith, we have peace with God through our Lord Jesus Christ." This is the heart and soul of piety. Believers do not need to worry about their status with God because they are justified by faith.

Sanctification is the process by which the believer increasingly becomes conformed to Christ in heart, conduct, and devotion to God. It is the continual

---

34. Institutes, 3.11.1.

35. John Calvin, *Sermons on Galatians,* trans. Kathy Childress (Edinburgh: Banner of Truth Trust, 1997), 2:17–18. Hereafter, *Sermon on Galatians* text.

36. Institutes, 3.11.2.

37. Ibid.

38. Institutes, 3.11.1, 3.15.7.

39. Institutes, 3.13.1.

remaking of the believer by the Holy Spirit, the increasing consecration of body and soul to God.[40] In sanctification, the believer offers himself to God. This does not come without great struggle and slow progress; it requires cleansing from the pollution of the flesh and renouncing of the world.[41] It demands repentance, mortification, and daily conversion.

Justification and sanctification are inseparable, Calvin says. To separate one from the other is to tear Christ in pieces;[42] it is like trying to separate the sun's light from the heat that light generates.[43] Believers are justified for the purpose of worshiping God in holiness of life.[44]

Ecclesiological Dimensions

Calvin's view of piety also contains a number of ecclesiological dimensions, including:

• *Piety through the church.* Calvin's piety is rooted in the Word and nurtured in the church. While breaking with the clericalism and absolutism of Rome, Calvin nonetheless maintains a high view of the church.[45] Believers are engrafted into Christ *and* His church because spiritual growth happens within the

---

40. Institutes, 1.7.5.

41. *Commentary* on John 17:17–19.

42. Institutes, 3.11.6.

43. *Sermon* on Galatians 2:17–18.

44. *Commentary* on Romans 6:2.

45. Institutes, 4.1.1, 3–4; cf. Joel R. Beeke, "Glorious Things of Thee Are Spoken: The Doctrine of the Church," in *Onward, Christian Soldiers: Protestants Affirm the Church,* ed. Don Kistler (Morgan, Pa.: Soli Deo Gloria, 1999), 23–25.

church. The church is mother, educator, and nour-
isher of every believer, for the Holy Spirit acts in
her. Believers cultivate piety by the Spirit through
the church's teaching ministry, progressing from
spiritual infancy to adolescence to full manhood in
Christ. They do not graduate from the church until
they die.[46] This lifelong education is offered within
an atmosphere of genuine piety in which believers
love and care for one another under the headship of
Christ.[47] Such education encourages the growth of
one another's gifts and love because it is "constrained
to borrow from others."[48]

Progress in piety is impossible apart from the
church, for piety is fostered by the communion of
saints. Within the church, believers "cleave to each
other in the mutual distribution of gifts."[49] Each
member has his own place and gifts to use within the
body.[50] Ideally, the entire body uses these gifts in symmetry and proportion, ever reforming and growing
toward perfection.[51]

• *Piety of the Word.* The Word of God is central to
the development of Christian piety in the believer.
Calvin's relational model explains how.

True religion is a dialogue between God and man.
The part of the dialogue that God initiates is revela-

---

46. Institutes, 4.1.4–5.
47. *Commentary* on Psalm 20:9.
48. *Commentary* on Romans 12:6.
49. *Commentary* on 1 Corinthians 12:12.
50. *Commentary* on 1 Corinthians 4:7.
51. *Commentary* on Ephesians 4:12.

Farel preaching in the market-place of Neuchâtel

tion, wherein He comes down to meet us, address us, and make Himself known to us in the preaching of the Word. The other part of the dialogue is man's response to God's revelation. This response, which includes trust, adoration, and godly fear, is what Calvin calls piety.

The preaching of the Word saves us and preserves us as the Spirit enables us to appropriate the blood of Christ and respond to Him with reverential love. By the Spirit-empowered preaching of men, "the renewal of the saints is accomplished and the body of Christ is edified," Calvin says.[52]

Furthermore, Calvin teaches that the preaching of the Word is our spiritual food and our medicine for spiritual health. With the Spirit's blessing, ministers are spiritual physicians who apply the Word to our

---

52. *Commentary* on Psalm 18:31; 1 Corinthians 13:12; Institutes, 4.1.5, 4.3.2.

souls as earthly physicians apply medicine to our
bodies. Using the Word, these spiritual doctors diag-
nose, prescribe for, and cure spiritual disease in those
plagued by sin and death. The preached Word is used
as an instrument to heal, cleanse, and make fruitful
our disease-prone souls.[53] The Spirit, or the "internal minister," promotes piety by using the "external
minister" to preach the Word. As Calvin says, the
external minister "holds forth the vocal word and
it is received by the ears," but the internal minister
"truly communicates the thing proclaimed . . . that
is Christ."[54]

• *Piety in the sacraments.* Calvin defines the sacraments
as testimonies "of divine grace toward us, confirmed
by an outward sign, with mutual attestation of
our piety toward him."[55] Thus, the sacraments are
"exercises of piety." They foster and strengthen our
faith, and help us offer ourselves as living sacrifices
to God.

In the sacraments, God accommodates Himself to
our weakness, Calvin says. He comes to His people
in the sacraments, encourages them, enables them to
know Christ better, builds them up, and nourishes

---

53. John Calvin, *Sermons of M. John Calvin, on the Epistles of S. Paule
to Timothie and Titus,* trans. L. T. (1579; reprint facsimile, Edinburgh:
Banner of Truth Trust, 1983), 1 Timothy 1:8–11.

54. John Calvin, *Calvin: Theological Treatises,* ed. J. K. S. Reid
(Philadelphia: Westminster Press, 1954), 173. Cf. Brian Armstrong,
"The Role of the Holy Spirit in Calvin's Teaching on the Ministry,"
Calvin and the Holy Spirit, ed. P. DeKlerk (Grand Rapids: Calvin Stud-
ies Society, 1989), 99–111.

55. Institutes, 4.14.1.

them in Him. Baptism promotes piety as a symbol of how believers are engrafted into Christ, renewed by the Spirit, and adopted into the family of the heavenly Father.[56] Likewise, the Lord's Supper shows how His adopted children are fed by their loving Father. Calvin loves to refer to the Supper as nourishment for the soul. "The signs are bread and wine which represent for us the invisible food that we receive from the flesh and blood of Christ," he writes. "Christ is the only food of our soul, and therefore our heavenly Father invites us to Christ, that refreshed by partaking of him, we may repeatedly gather strength until we shall have reached heavenly immortality."[57]

Calvin teaches that Christ gives Himself, not just His benefits, to us in the Supper. Christ also makes us part of His body as He gives us Himself. Calvin cannot precisely explain how that happens in the Supper, for it is better experienced than explained.[58] However, he does say that Christ does not leave heaven to enter the bread. Rather, by the Spirit's work within us, we are called to lift our hearts up to heaven, where Christ is, and not cling to the external bread and wine.

When we meet Christ in the sacraments, we grow in grace; that is why they are called means of grace. The sacraments therefore encourage us in our progress toward heaven. They promote confidence in God's promises through Christ's "signified and

---

56. Institutes, 4.16.9; Ronald S. Wallace, *Calvin's Doctrine of the Word and Sacrament* (London: Oliver and Boyd, 1953), 175–183. Cf. H. O. Old, *The Shaping of the Reformed Baptismal Rite in the Sixteenth Century* (Grand Rapids: Eerdmans, 1992).

57. Institutes, 4.17.8–12.

58. Institutes, 4.17.24, 33.

sealed" redemptive death. Since they are covenants, they contain promises by which "consciences may be roused to an assurance of salvation," Calvin says.[59]

Finally, the sacraments promote piety by prompting us to thank and praise God for His abundant grace. We offer this sacrifice of gratitude in response to Christ's sacrifice for us. We surrender our lives in light of the heavenly banquet God spreads for us in the Supper. By the Spirit's grace, the Supper enables us as a royal priesthood to offer ourselves as living sacrifices of praise and thanksgiving to God.[60] The Lord's Supper thus prompts both piety of grace received and piety of gratitude given.[61]

• *Piety in the Psalter.* Calvin views the book of Psalms as the canonical manual of piety. In the preface to his five-volume commentary on the Psalms—his largest exposition of any Bible book—Calvin writes: "There is no other book in which we are more perfectly taught the right manner of praising God, or in which we are more powerfully stirred up to the performance of this exercise of piety."[62] Calvin's preoccupation with the Psalter was motivated by his belief that the book of Psalms teaches and inspires genuine piety by (1) teaching us our need for God; (2) serving as our sung creed; (3) demonstrating God's amazing good-

---

59. *Commentary* on 1 Corinthians 11:25.

60. Institutes, 4.18.13.

61. "Calvin's Eucharistic Piety," in *The Legacy of John Calvin,* ed. David Foxgrover (Grand Rapids: CRC, 2000), 53.

62. *CO* 31:19; translation taken from Barbara Pitkin, "Imitation of David: David as a Paradigm for Faith in Calvin's Exegesis of the Psalms," *Sixteenth Century Journal,* 24, no. 4 (1993): 847.

ness; (4) fostering prayer; (5) providing a vehicle for communal worship; (6) showing the depth of communion we may enjoy with God; and (7) covering the full range of spiritual experience, including faith and unbelief, joy in God and sorrow over sin, and divine presence and divine desertion. As Calvin says, the psalms are "an anatomy of all parts of the soul."[63]

Calvin immersed himself in the book of Psalms for twenty-five years as a commentator, preacher, biblical scholar, and worship leader.[64] Early on, he began work on metrical versions of psalms to be used in public worship. Later, he recruited the talents of men such as Clement Marot, Louis Bourgeois, and Theodore Beza to produce the Genevan Psalter. Two years before his death, Calvin was delighted to see its first complete edition.[65]

The Genevan Psalter, a remarkable collection of 125 melodies, clearly expresses Calvin's convictions

---

63. *Commentary* on the Psalms, 1:xxxix. See James A. De Jong, "An Anatomy of All Parts of the Soul: Insights into Calvin's Spirituality from His Psalms Commentary," in *Calvinus Sacrae Scripturae Professor* (Grand Rapids: Eerdmans, 1994), 1–14.

64. John Walchenbach, "The Influence of David and the Psalms on the Life and Thought of John Calvin" (Th.M. thesis, Pittsburgh Theological Seminary, 1969).

65. More than 30,000 copies of the first complete, 500-page Genevan Psalter were printed by more than fifty different French and Swiss publishers in the first year, and at least 27,400 copies were published in Geneva in the first few months (Jeffrey T. VanderWilt, "John Calvin's Theology of Liturgical Song," *Christian Scholar's Review* 25 [1996]: 67. Cf. John Witvliet, "The Spirituality of the Psalter: Metrical Psalms in Liturgy and Life in Calvin's Geneva," in *Calvin Study Society Papers, 1995–1997,* ed. David Foxgrover [Grand Rapids: CRC, 1998], 93–117).

CLÉMENT MAROT (1496–1544)

French poet who helped with the Genevan Psalter

that piety is best promoted when priority is given to
text over tune, while recognizing that psalms deserve
their own music. Since music should help the reception of the Word, Calvin says, it should be "weighty,
dignified, majestic, and modest"—fitting attributes
for the benefit of a sinful creature in the presence
of God.[66] This protects the sovereignty of God in
worship and promotes proper conformity between
the believer's inward disposition and his outward
confession.

Psalm-singing is one of the four principal acts
of church worship, Calvin believed. He saw it as an
extension of prayer. Also, Calvin thought that corporate singing subdued the fallen heart and retrained
wayward affections in the way of piety. Like preaching and the sacraments, psalm-singing disciplines
the heart's affections in the school of faith and lifts
the believer to God. It also amplifies the effect of
the Word upon the heart and multiplies the spiritual
energy of the church.[67] With the Spirit's direction,
psalm-singing tunes the hearts of believers for glory.

The Genevan Psalter was an integral part of Calvinist worship for centuries. It set the standard for
succeeding French Reformed psalm books, as well as
those in English, Dutch, German, and Hungarian. As
a devotional book, it warmed the hearts of thousands,
but the people who sang from it understood that its

66. Preface to the Genevan Psalter (1562). Charles Garside Jr.,
The Origins of Calvin's Theology of Music: 1536–1543 (Philadelphia: The
American Philosophical Society, 1979), 32–33.

67. *CO* 10:12; cited in Garside, *The Origins of Calvin's Theology of
Music,* 10.

power was not in the book or its words, but in the Spirit who impressed those words on their hearts.

The Genevan Psalter promoted piety by stimulating a spirituality of the Word that was corporate and liturgical, and that broke down the distinction between liturgy and life. The Calvinists freely sang psalms not only in their churches but also in homes and workplaces, on the streets, and in the fields.[68] The singing of psalms became a "means of Huguenot self-identification."[69] In fact, this pious exercise became a cultural emblem. T. Hartley Hall writes, "In scriptural or metrical versions, the Psalms, together with the stately tunes to which they were early set, are clearly the heart and soul of Reformed piety."[70]

Practical Dimensions

Although Calvin views the church as the nursery of piety, he also emphasizes the need for personal piety. The Christian strives for piety because he loves righteousness, longs to live to God's glory, and delights to obey God's rule of righteousness set forth in Scripture.[71] For Calvin, such piety "is the beginning,

---

68. Witvliet, "The Spirituality of the Psalter," 117.

69. W. Stanford Reid, "The Battle Hymns of the Lord: Calvinist Psalmody of the Sixteenth Century," in *Sixteenth Century Essays and Studies,* ed. C. S. Meyer (St. Louis: Foundation for Reformation Research, 1971), 2:47.

70. T. Hartley Hall, "The Shape of Reformed Piety," in Robin Maas and Gabriel O'Donnell, *Spiritual Traditions for the Contemporary Church* (Nashville: Abingdon Press, 1990), 215. Cf. Reid, "The Battle Hymns of the Lord," 2:36–54.

71. Institutes, 3.6.2.

middle, and end of Christian living."[72] Here is a summary of what Calvin says on pious Christian living in Book 3 of the *Institutes* of 1559:[73]

• *Prayer.* Prayer is the principal and perpetual exercise of faith and the chief element of piety.[74] As the believer comes to God in prayer, he receives a sense of God's gracious character even as he offers praises to God and asks for His faithfulness. Prayer encourages piety both privately and corporately.[75]

For Calvin, prayer is the essence of the Christian life. It is a precious gift, not an academic problem.[76] For this reason, he devotes the second-longest chapter of the *Institutes* (Book 3, Chapter 20) to prayer, providing six purposes for it: (1) to fly to God with every need and gain from Him what is lacking in ourselves to live the Christian life; (2) to learn to desire wholeheartedly only what is right as we place all our petitions before God; (3) to become prepared to receive God's benefits and responses to our peti-

---

72. *Commentary* on 1 Timothy 4:7–8.

73. Chapters 6–10 of Book 3 were first translated into English in 1549 as *The Life and Conversation of a Christian Man* and have been reprinted often as *The Golden Booklet of the True Christian Life*.

74. See R. D. Loggie, "Chief Exercise of Faith: An Exposition of Calvin's Doctrine of Prayer," *Hartford Quarterly,* 5 (1965): 65–81, and H. W. Maurer, "An Examination of Form and Content in John Calvin's Prayers" (Ph.D. dissertation, University of Edinburgh, 1960).

75. Cf. Thomas A. Lambert, "Preaching, Praying, and Policing the Reform in Sixteenth Century Geneva" (Ph.D. dissertation, University of Wisconsin-Madison, 1998), 393–480.

76. Charles Partee, "Prayer as the Practice of Predestination," in *Calvinus Servus Christi,* ed. Wilhelm H. Neuser (Budapest: Pressabteilung des Raday-Kollegiums, 1988), 246.

tions with humble gratitude; (4) to be led to meditate on God's kindness to us as we receive what we have asked for; (5) to cultivate the proper spirit of delight for God's answers in prayer; and (6) to confirm God's faithful providence so that we may glorify Him and trust in His present help more readily as we witness Him regularly answering our prayers.[77]

Right prayer is governed by rules, Calvin says. These include praying with a heartfelt sense of reverence; a heartfelt sense of need and repentance; a heartfelt sense of humility and trust in God; and a heartfelt sense of confident hope. All four rules are repeatedly violated by even the holiest of God's people. Nevertheless, for Christ's sake, God does not desert the pious but has mercy for them.[78]

• *Repentance.* Repentance is the fruit of faith and prayer. Like Martin Luther, Calvin sees repentance as a lifelong process. He says that repentance is not merely the start of the Christian life; it *is* the Christian life. It involves confession of sin as well as growth in holiness. Repentance is the lifelong response of the believer to the gospel in outward life, mind, heart, attitude, and will.[79]

Repentance begins with turning to God from the heart because of a pure, earnest fear of Him. It involves dying to self and sin (mortification) and coming alive to righteousness (vivification) in Christ.[80] Mortification is the means to vivification, which

---

77. Institutes, 3.20.3.

78. Institutes, 3.20.4–16.

79. Institutes, 3.3.1–2, 6, 18, 20.

80. Institutes, 3.3.5, 9.

Calvin defines as "the desire to live in a holy and devoted manner, a desire arising from rebirth; as if it were said that man dies to himself that he may begin to live to God."[81]

• *Self-denial and cross-bearing.* Self-denial is the sacrificial dimension of piety, a fruit of the believer's union with Christ. It includes (1) realizing that we belong to God rather than to ourselves, (2) desiring to orient our entire lives toward God, and (3) yielding ourselves and all that we possess to God as living sacrifices.

While self-denial focuses on inward conformity to Christ, cross-bearing centers on outward Christlikeness. Those who are in fellowship with Christ must prepare themselves for a hard, toilsome life filled with many kinds of evil, Calvin says. This is not simply due to sin's effect on this fallen world, but also because of the believer's union with Christ. Because His life was a perpetual cross, ours also must include suffering.[82] We not only participate in the benefits of His atoning work on the cross, we also experience the Spirit's work of transforming us into the image of Christ.[83]

Cross-bearing tests piety, Calvin says. Through cross-bearing, we are roused to hope, trained in patience, instructed in obedience, and chastened in

---

81. Institutes, 3.3.3; cf. Randall C. Gleason, *John Calvin and John Owen on Mortification: A Comparative Study in Reformed Spirituality* (New York: Peter Lang, 1995), 61.

82. Richard C. Gamble, "Calvin and Sixteenth-Century Spirituality," in *Calvin Studies Society Papers,* 34–35.

83. Institutes, 3.8.1–2.

pride. Cross-bearing is our medicine and our chastise-
ment; it reveals the feebleness of our flesh and teaches
us to suffer for the sake of righteousness.[84]

• *The present and future life.* Through cross-bearing, we
learn contempt for the present life when compared
with the blessings of heaven. This life is nothing
compared with what is to come; it is like smoke or
a shadow. "If heaven is our homeland, what else is
the earth but our place of exile? If departure from the
world is entry into life, what else is the world but a
sepulcher?" Calvin asks.[85] "No one has made progress
in the school of Christ who does not joyfully await the
day of death and final resurrection," he concludes.[86]

Typically, Calvin uses the *complexio oppositorum*
when explaining the Christian's relation to this world,
presenting opposites to find a middle way between
them. Thus, on the one hand, cross-bearing crucifies
us to the world and the world to us. On the other
hand, the devout Christian enjoys this present life,
albeit with due restraint and moderation, for he is
taught to use things in this world for the purpose that
God intended for them. Calvin was no ascetic; he
enjoyed good literature, good food, and the beauties
of nature. But he rejected all forms of earthly excess.
The believer is called to Christlike moderation, which
includes modesty, prudence, avoidance of display,
and contentment with our lot.[87] The hope of the life

---

84. Institutes, 3.8.3–9.

85. Institutes, 3.9.4.

86. Institutes, 3.9.5.

87. Ronald S. Wallace, *Calvin's Doctrine of the Christian Life* (London: Oliver & Boyd, 1959), 170–195.

to come gives purpose to and enjoyment of our present life. This life is always straining after a better, heavenly life.[88]

• *Obedience.* For Calvin, unconditional obedience to God's will is the essence of piety. Piety links love, freedom, and discipline by subjecting all to the will and Word of God.[89] Love is the overarching principle that prevents piety from degenerating into legalism. At the same time, law provides the content for love.

Piety includes rules that govern the believer's responses. Privately, adherence to these rules takes the form of self-denial; publicly, they are expressed in the exercise of church discipline, as Calvin implemented in Geneva. In either case, the glory of God compels disciplined obedience. For Calvin, the pious Christian is neither weak nor passive but dynamically active in the pursuit of obedience—much like a distance runner, a diligent scholar, or a heroic warrior, submitting to God's will.[90]

Calvin's Example

Calvin strove to live a life of genuine piety himself—theologically, ecclesiastically, and practically.[91] He shows us the piety of a warm-hearted Reformed

---

88. Institutes, 3.9.3.

89. Lionel Greve, "John Calvin, William Perkins and John Wesley: An Examination of the Origin and Nature of Pietism" (Ph.D. dissertation, Hartford Seminary Foundation, 1975), 20.

90. John S. Leith, *John Calvin's Doctrine of the Christian Life* (Louisville: Westminster/John Knox Press, 1989), 82–86.

91. See *Selected Works of Calvin,* ed. and trans. Henry Beveridge (Grand Rapids: Baker, 1983), 1:c. For more on piety in Calvin's life,

The Reformation Wall in Geneva

Guillaume Farel, John Calvin,
Theodore Beza, John Knox

theologian who speaks from the heart. Having tasted
the goodness and grace of God in Jesus Christ, he pursued piety by seeking to know and do God's will every
day. He communed with Christ; practiced repentance,
self-denial, and cross-bearing; and was involved in
vigorous social improvements.[92] His theology worked
itself out in heartfelt, Christ-centered piety.[93]

---

see Ford Lewis Battles, *The Piety of John Calvin* (Grand Rapids: Baker,
1978), 16–20.

92. Merwyn Johnson, "Calvin's Ethical Legacy," in *The Legacy of
John Calvin,* 79–83.

93. Cf. Erroll Hulse, "The Preacher and Piety," in *The Preacher
and Preaching,* ed. Samuel T. Logan, Jr. (Phillipsburg, N.J.: P&R,
1986), 71.

For Calvin and the Calvinists of sixteenth-century Europe, doctrine and prayer, as well as faith and worship, were integrally connected. The Reformation included a reform of piety, or spirituality, as much as a reform of theology. The spirituality that had been cloistered behind monastery walls for centuries had broken down; medieval spirituality was reduced to a celibate, ascetic, and penitential devotion in the convent or monastery. Calvin helped Christians understand piety in terms of living and acting every day according to God's will (Rom. 12:1–2) in the midst of human society. Through his influence, Calvinistic spirituality focused on how one lived the Christian life in the family, the fields, the workshop, and the marketplace.[94]

Calvin helped Protestants change the entire focus of the Christian life. His piety, and that of his followers, served as a comprehensive pattern for the Reformation. May God enable us also to live pious lives to His glory. Only then will we be genuine sons and daughters of the Calvinistic Reformation.

---

94. Hughes Oliphant Old, "What is Reformed Spirituality? Played Over Again Lightly," in *Calvin Studies VII*, ed. J. H. Leith (Davidson, N.C.: n.p., 1994), 61.

SECTION ONE

The Definition and Importance of Piety

1

Piety Essential for Knowing God[1]

Now, the knowledge of God, as I understand it, is that by which we not only conceive that there is a God but also grasp what befits us and is proper to his glory—in fine, what is to our advantage to know of him. Indeed, we shall not say that, properly speaking, God is known where there is no religion or piety. Here I do not yet touch on the sort of knowledge with which men, in themselves lost and accursed, apprehend God the Redeemer in Christ the Mediator; but I speak only of the primal and simple knowledge to which the very order of nature would have led us if Adam had remained upright. In this ruin of mankind no one now experiences God either as Father or as Author of salvation, or favorable in any way, until Christ the Mediator comes forward to reconcile him to us. Nevertheless, it is one thing to feel that God as our Maker supports us by his power, governs us by his providence, nourishes us by his goodness, and attends us with all sorts of blessings—and another thing to embrace the grace of reconciliation offered to us in Christ. First, as much in the fashioning of the universe as in the general teaching of Scripture the

---

1. Institutes 1.2.1.

Lord shows himself to be simply the Creator. Then in the face of Christ (cf. 2 Cor. 4:6) he shows himself the Redeemer. Of the resulting twofold knowledge of God we shall now discuss the first aspect; the second will be dealt with in its proper place.

Moreover, although our mind cannot apprehend God without rendering some honor to him, it will not suffice simply to hold that there is One whom all ought to honor and adore, unless we are also persuaded that he is the fountain of every good, and that we must seek nothing elsewhere than in him. This I take to mean that not only does he sustain this universe (as he once founded it) by his boundless might, regulate it by his wisdom, preserve it by his goodness, and especially rule mankind by his righteousness and judgment, bear with it in his mercy, watch over it by his protection; but also that no drop will be found either of wisdom and light, or of righteousness or power or rectitude, or of genuine truth, that does not flow from him, and of which he is not the cause. Thus we may learn to await and seek all these things from him, and thankfully to ascribe them, once received, to him. For this sense of the powers of God is for us a fit teacher of piety, from which religion is born. I call "piety" that reverence joined with love of God that the knowledge of his benefits induces. For until men recognize that they owe everything to God, that they are nourished by his fatherly care, that he is the Author of their every good, that they should seek nothing beyond him—they will never yield him willing service. Nay, unless they establish their complete happiness in him, they will never give themselves truly and sincerely to him.

2

—•⟩•‹(•)›•‹—

Piety as "the Soul of Life"[1]

"According as his divine power hath given unto
us all things that pertain unto life and godliness,
through the knowledge of him that hath called us
to glory and virtue."

—2 Peter 1:3

That pertain to life and godliness, or as to life and godliness. Some think that the present life is meant here, as godliness follows as the more excellent gift, as though by those two words Peter intended to prove how beneficent and bountiful God is towards the faithful, that he brought them to light, that he supplies them with all things necessary for the preservation of an earthly life, and that he has also renewed them to a spiritual life by adorning them with godliness. But this distinction is foreign to the mind of Peter, for as soon as he mentioned life, he immediately added godliness, which is, as it were, its soul;[2] for God then truly gives us life, when he renews us unto the obedience of righteousness. So Peter does not speak here of the

---

1. *Commentary* on 2 Peter 1:3.

2. The Johnston translation from the Torrance edition translates this as "he immediately adds godliness [or piety, *pietas*] as it were *the soul of life*" (emphasis added)—from which the title of this book is drawn (Grand Rapids: Eerdmans, 1963).

natural gifts of God, but only mentions those things that he confers peculiarly on his own elect above the common order of nature.

That we are born men, that we are endued with reason and knowledge, that our life is supplied with necessary support—all this is indeed from God. As however men, being perverted in their minds and ungrateful, do not regard these various things, which are called the gifts of nature, among God's benefits, the common condition of human life is not here referred to, but the peculiar endowments of the new and spiritual life, which derive their origin from the kingdom of Christ. But since everything necessary for godliness and salvation is to be deemed among the supernatural gifts of God, let men learn to arrogate nothing to themselves, but humbly ask of God whatever they see they are wanting in, and to ascribe to him whatever good they may have. For Peter here, by attributing the whole of godliness, and helps to salvation, to the divine power of Christ, takes them away from the common nature of men, so that he leaves to us not even the least particle of any virtue or merit.

Through the knowledge of him. He now describes the manner in which God makes us partakers of so great blessings, even by making himself known to us by the gospel. For the knowledge of God is the beginning of life and the first entrance into godliness. In short, spiritual gifts cannot be given for salvation, until, being illuminated by the doctrine of the gospel, we are led to know God. But he makes God the author of this knowledge, because we never go to him except when called. Hence the effectual cause of faith is not the perspicacity of our mind, but the calling of God. And he speaks not of the outward calling only, which is in itself ineffectual; but of the inward calling, effected by the hidden power of the Spirit, when God not only sounds in our ears by the voice of man, but draws inwardly our hearts to himself by his own Spirit.

MELCHIOR WOLMAR (1497–1560)

French Scholar, tutor of both Calvin and Beza. His influence upon these two extended beyond their Greek studies to Reformation truth.

3

Piety in Practice[1]

"Exercise thyself rather unto godliness. For bodily exercise profiteth little; but godliness is profitable unto all things, having promise of the life that now is, and of that which is to come."

—1 Timothy 4:7b–8

Exercise thyself to godliness. After having instructed him [Timothy] as to doctrine, what it ought to be, he now also admonishes him what kind of example he ought to give to others. He says that he ought to be employed in "godliness." For when he says, "Exercise thyself," he means that this is his proper occupation, his labor, his chief care. [It is] as if he had said, "There is no reason why you should weary yourself to no purpose about other matters; you will do what is of the highest importance, if you devote yourself with all your zeal, and with all your ability, to godliness alone." By the word *godliness,* he means the spiritual worship of God, which consists in purity of conscience—which is still more evident from what follows, when it is contrasted with bodily exercise....

But godliness is profitable for all things. That is, he who has godliness wants nothing, though he has

---

1. *Commentary* on 1 Timothy 4:7b–8.

not those little aids [found in bodily exercise]. For godliness alone is able to conduct a man to complete perfection. It is the beginning, the middle, and the end of Christian life, and, therefore, where that is entire, nothing is imperfect.

Let the meaning be thus summed up. "We ought to apply ourselves altogether to piety alone, because when we have once attained it, God asks nothing more from us, and we ought to give attention to bodily exercises in such a manner as not to hinder or retard the practice of godliness."

SECTION TWO

Piety's Supreme Goal,
Soli Deo Gloria

4

Piety's Zeal for God[1]

We seek not the things that are ours but those that are of the Lord's will and will serve to advance his glory. This is also evidence of great progress: that, almost forgetful of ourselves, surely subordinating our self-concern, we try faithfully to devote our zeal to God and his commandments. For when Scripture bids us leave off self-concern, it not only erases from our minds the yearning to possess, the desire for power, and the favor of men, but it also uproots ambition and all craving for human glory and other more secret plagues. Accordingly, the Christian must surely be so disposed and minded that he feels within himself it is with God he has to deal throughout his life. In this way, as he will refer all he has to God's decision and judgment, so will he refer his whole intention of mind scrupulously to him. For he who has learned to look to God in all things that he must do, at the same time avoids all vain thoughts. This, then, is that denial of self that Christ enjoins with such great earnestness on his disciples at the outset of their service (cf. Matt. 16:24). When it has once taken possession of their hearts, it leaves no place at all first either to pride, or arrogance, or ostentation; then either to avarice, or desire, or lasciviousness, or effeminacy, or to other

---

1. Institutes 3.7.2.

evils that our self-love spawns (cf. 2 Tim. 3:2–5). On the other hand, wherever denial of ourselves does not reign, there either the foulest vices rage without shame or, if there is any semblance of virtue, it is vitiated by depraved lusting after glory. Show me a man, if you can, who, unless he has according to the commandment of the Lord renounced himself, would freely exercise goodness among men. For all who have not been possessed with this feeling have at least followed virtue for the sake of praise....

Yet we have still not clearly explained how many and how great are the obstacles that hinder man from a right course so long as he has not denied himself. For it was once truly said: "A world of vices is hidden in the soul of man." And you can find no other remedy than in denying yourself and giving up concern for yourself, and in turning your mind wholly to seek after those things that the Lord requires of you, and to seek them only because they are pleasing to him.

5

Piety's Progress[1]

"That he would give to you, according to the riches of his glory, to be strengthened with power through his Spirit in the inner man."
—Ephesians 3:16

That he would give to you. Paul wishes that the Ephesians should be *strengthened,* and yet he had already bestowed on their piety no mean commendation. But believers have never advanced so far as not to need further growth. The highest perfection of the godly in this life is an earnest desire to make progress. This *strengthening,* he tells us, is the work of the *Spirit,* so that it does not proceed from man's own ability. The increase, as well as the commencement, of everything good in us, comes from the Holy Spirit. That it is the gift of divine grace is evident from the expression used: "that he would give to you...." But let us unite with Paul in acknowledging that it is the "gift" of the grace of God, not only that we have begun to run well, but that we advance; not only that we have been born again, but that we grow from day to day.

According to the riches of his glory. These words are intended to express still more strongly the doctrine

---

1. *Commentary* on Ephesians 3:16.

of divine grace. They may be explained in two ways: either "according to his glorious riches," or "according to his rich and abundant glory." The word *glory* will thus be put for *mercy*, in accordance with an expression that he had formerly used: "to the praise of the glory of his grace" (Eph. 1:6). I prefer the latter view.

In the inner man. By *the inner man*, Paul means the soul, and whatever relates to the spiritual life of the soul; as the *outward* man denotes the body, with everything that belongs to it—health, honors, riches, vigor, beauty, and everything of that nature. "Though our outward man perish, yet our inward man is renewed day by day"; that is, if in worldly matters we decay, our spiritual life becomes more and more vigorous (2 Cor. 4:16). The prayer of Paul, that the saints may be *strengthened*, does not mean that they may be eminent and flourishing in the world, but that, with respect to the kingdom of God, their minds may be made strong by divine power.

6

Piety's Imperfection[1]

I do not insist that the moral life of a Christian man breathe nothing but the very gospel, yet this ought to be desired, and we must strive toward it. But I do not so strictly demand evangelical perfection that I would not acknowledge as a Christian one who has not yet attained it. For thus all would be excluded from the church, since no one is found who is not far removed from it, while many have advanced a little toward it whom it would nevertheless be unjust to cast away.

What then? Let that target be set before our eyes at which we are earnestly to aim. Let that goal be appointed toward which we should strive and struggle. For it is not lawful for you to divide things with God in such a manner that you undertake part of those things that are enjoined on you by his Word but omit part, according to your own judgment. For in the first place, he everywhere commends integrity as the chief part of worshiping him (Gen. 17:1; Ps. 41:12, etc.). By this word he means a sincere simplicity of mind, free from guile and feigning, the opposite of a double heart. It is as if it were said that the beginning of right living is spiritual, where the inner feeling of the mind is unfeignedly dedicated to God for the cultivation of holiness and righteousness.

---

1. Institutes 3.6.5.

But no one in this earthly prison of the body has sufficient strength to press on with due eagerness, and weakness so weighs down the greater number that, with wavering and limping and even creeping along the ground, they move at a feeble rate. Let each one of us, then, proceed according to the measure of his puny capacity and set out on the journey we have begun. No one shall set out so inauspiciously as not daily to make some headway, though it be slight. Therefore, let us not cease so to act that we may make some unceasing progress in the way of the Lord. And let us not despair at the slightness of our success, for even though attainment may not correspond to desire, when today outstrips yesterday the effort is not lost. Only let us look toward our mark with sincere simplicity and aspire to our goal, not fondly flattering ourselves nor excusing our own evil deeds, but with continuous effort striving toward this end: that we may surpass ourselves in goodness until we attain to goodness itself. It is this, indeed, that through the whole course of life we seek and follow. But we shall attain it only when we have cast off the weakness of the body and are received into full fellowship with him.

SECTION THREE

Theological Dimensions

- *Piety's Profound Root: Mystical Union* (chapters 7–9)

- *Piety's Double Bond: The Spirit and Faith* (chapters 10–12)

- *Piety's Double Cleansing: Justification and Sanctification* (chapters 13–15)

7

Relishing an
Incomprehensible Union[1]

> "For this cause shall a man leave father and
> mother, and be joined to his wife, and they shall
> be two in one flesh. This is a great secret. Yes, I
> say, in Christ and in the church."
> —Ephesians 5:31–32

When a man speaks of the spiritual life that we have
with the Son of God, he is speaking of something
above nature. For although we do not have any
worthiness or excellency when we come out of our
mother's womb, yet there always remains some
imprint and image of God. And yet for all that we
are so cursed in our nature, and so miserable, that
we are called even deceased and dead. And that is
the reason why our Lord Jesus Christ says that the
hour is come that the dead, which are like rotting
carcasses in the grave, shall hear the voice of the
Son of God (John 5:25). And St. Paul has also said
in Ephesians 2 that when we are reformed by our
Lord Jesus Christ, then we live, whereas before we
were dead in our sins and transgressions, because
we receive that from our father Adam, as it were by

---

1. Sermon on Ephesians 5:31–33.

inheritance. The way therefore that we are of Jesus Christ's flesh, and bone of his bone, is that we are incorporated into him.

St. Paul also uses the similitude of grafting (Rom. 6:5). Just as a graft that is set into a stock takes its sustenance from the same, so must we, by being grafted into our Lord Jesus Christ. It is true that we do not yet bring forth good fruit of ourselves, for his purpose here is only to show that a branch, being broken, withers if it is left in that state, but receives sap and nourishment from the root if it is grafted into another. Even so it is with us; that is to say, if we continue such as we are by nature, then we are in death, because we are separated from our Lord Jesus Christ. But if we are incorporated into him, and it pleases him to communicate himself to us, then we feel in very deed that bread no more nourishes us when we eat it, nor wine strengthens us better when we drink it, than we receive life and vigor by the body and blood of our Lord Jesus Christ.

Now that this is a high mystery every man is able to judge for himself. When we have debated very much and searched our hearts in the matter, is there any of us that can comprehend how we are joined to our Lord Jesus Christ, and how we are made one with him, so that we can assure ourselves and be convinced that we shall in this way be partakers of the glory of God, and that even today we live in our Lord Jesus Christ? As also he said, "Be of good cheer, for as I live, you shall live also" (John 14:19). Can this, I say, enter into such a small space as our natural reason is? Certainly not! And that is the reason why many men cannot admit this point, that we are the flesh of Jesus Christ, and bone of his bones. They content themselves with their own imaginations, which destroy the grace of God. St. Paul was not able to express that grace but rather showed us that it ought to ravish our minds in astonishment.

ERASMUS OF ROTTERDAM (1466/1469–1536)

Famous Dutch scholar whom Calvin met while in Basel. Although Erasmus never embraced Protestant convictions, he influenced many of the Reformers and his work on New Testament and concern with abuses within the Roman Catholic Church added much leverage to the Reformation.

8

Enjoying a Great Mystery[1]

> "For this cause shall a man leave father and mother, and be joined to his wife, and they shall be two in one flesh. This is a great secret. Yes, I say, in Christ and in the church."
> —Ephesians 5:31–32

Many may happen to have a vague and, as it were, a profane imagination that we are joined to our Lord Jesus Christ—that is to say, that we are saved by his grace. But the Scripture goes much further, and though there were no more than this saying, that it is "a great mystery," yet let us beware of limiting it according to our own fancy, for it would be just like making St. Paul a liar.

All such as despise this spiritual union that we have with our Lord Jesus Christ wish to show that there is no such secret or wonderful power of God, or anything else that we hear spoken of in this passage. And the Holy Spirit uses such language to humble us and afterwards to lift us up again. Therefore on the one hand we must confess that all the wisdom and understanding we have fails us in that respect; and afterward we are raised up again, because we hear our

---

1. Sermon on Ephesians 5:31–33.

Lord Jesus Christ call us to himself and tell us that we are so joined to him that he does not have anything of his own that he does not share with us, and of which he will not have us to be partakers. Therefore, if we find here any contradictions, and it puzzles us to wonder how it is possible that our Lord Jesus Christ who is in heaven should nourish us with his own substance, so that his body should be our meat and his blood our drink—I say, if we fall into such fancies, we must repulse them all with what is said here, namely, that it is a secret and we must rebuke our own folly and rashness in trying to measure what is infinite. Our Lord shows us that when he has joined us to his only Son, he has done so high and profound a work as overtops all our capacity to understand. Seeing it is so, let us always conclude that although we find it a strange matter, yet we must acquiesce in what is spoken by God himself, especially when he says that he will work in so high a fashion that we shall be utterly ravished by it.

Wherefore let us learn generally from this passage that all the spiritual benefits we receive through our Lord Jesus Christ, by which to attain to the heavenly life, are and do proceed from the said fountain of the incomprehensible wisdom of God, so that it is not for us to be so foolishly presumptuous as to say, "I will know what is in it; and then I shall see what pleases me." Let us restrain ourselves from such presumption, for it will make us unworthy of this mystery of faith, because it is a statement that signifies a great secret. The end, I say, at which we must begin, if we wish Jesus Christ to benefit us, and if we desire to be partakers of all his graces, is to understand that

God has so worked in our salvation as to render it a mystery.... It is a great secret, St. Paul says, that God was manifested in the flesh (1 Tim. 3:16). For what a distance there is between God and man! We are but vermin and rottenness, and God's majesty is so high that no man can say what it is or conceive a hundredth part of it, but we are bound to be ravished with astonishment at it.

Seeing then that God has so conjoined himself with us that he is the true Emmanuel (as he is called in Isaiah, Isa. 7:14), and that the things that seem to be so far apart are joined together in the person of our Lord Jesus Christ, let us thereupon conclude that there is nothing but mysteries and secrets in all the grace we receive from our God, and especially in our incorporation into our Lord Jesus Christ, who having taken our nature on him and clothed himself with our flesh, will have us to be grafted into him, as into our root, to the end that we might be quickened by his Spirit and be partakers of his life, so that he has nothing reserved to himself alone, but will have everything imparted to us.

Do we then desire to receive our Lord Jesus Christ with all the benefits that he brings us, and through him to overcome all the temptations that can come before us? It is necessary for us to have a thorough taste of the things that the Scripture tells us and sets before us, and to give reverent credit to them, acknowledging that God works in us by our Lord Jesus Christ that the same may content us, even as we forsake all our natural understanding.

SIMON GRYNAEUS (1493–1541)

German Reformer, helped compose the First Helvetic Confession (1536). Calvin met him during his first visit to Basel, and the two remained very close friends and correspondents.

9

Eating the Living Bread[1]

> "I am the living bread which hath come down from heaven; if any man eat of this bread, he shall live for ever; and the bread which I shall give is my flesh, which I shall give for the life of the world."
>
> —John 6:51

I am the living bread. He [Jesus] often repeats the same thing because nothing is more necessary to be known, and every one feels in himself with what difficulty we are brought to believe it and how easily and quickly it passes away and is forgotten. We all desire life, but in seeking it, we foolishly and improperly wander about in circuitous roads, and when it is offered, the greater part disdainfully reject it. For who is there that does not contrive for himself life out of Christ? And how few are there who are satisfied with Christ alone! It is not a superfluous repetition, therefore, when Christ asserts so frequently that he alone is sufficient to give life. For he claims for himself the designation of *bread*, in order to tear from our hearts all fallacious hopes of living. Having formerly called himself *the bread of life*, he now calls himself *the living bread*, but in the same sense—namely, *life-giving bread*.

---

1. *Commentary* on John 6:51.

Which have come down from heaven. He frequently mentions his *coming down from heaven*, because spiritual and incorruptible life will not be found in this world, the fashion of which passes away and vanishes, but only in the heavenly kingdom of God.

If any man eat of this bread. Whenever he uses the word *eat,* he exhorts us to faith, which alone enables us to enjoy this bread, so as to derive life from it. Nor is it without good reason that he does so, for there are few who deign to stretch out their hand to put this bread to their mouth; even when the Lord puts it into their mouth, there are few who relish it, but some are filled with wind, and others…are dying of hunger through their own folly, while the food is close beside them.

The bread which I shall give is my flesh. As this secret power to bestow life, of which he has spoken, might be referred to his divine essence, he now comes down to the second step, and shows that this *life* is placed *in his flesh,* that it may be drawn out of it. It is, undoubtedly, a wonderful purpose of God that he has exhibited life to us in that *flesh,* where formerly there was nothing but the cause of death. And thus he provides for our weakness, when he does not call us above the clouds to enjoy life, but displays it on earth, in the same manner as if he were exalting us to the secrets of his kingdom. And yet, while he corrects the pride of our mind, he tries the humility and obedience of our faith when he enjoins those who would seek *life* to place reliance on his *flesh,* which is contemptible in its appearance.

But an objection is brought, that the flesh of Christ cannot give life, because it was liable to death, and because even now it is not immortal in itself; and next, that it does not at all belong to the nature of flesh to quicken souls. I reply, though this power comes from another source than from the flesh, still this is no reason why the designation may not accurately apply to it. For as the eternal word of God is the fountain of *life* (John 1:4), so his flesh, as a channel, conveys to us that *life* that dwells intrinsically, as we say, in his divinity. And in this sense it is called life-giving, because it conveys to us that life that it borrows for us from another quarter. This will not be difficult to understand, if we consider what is the cause of life—namely, righteousness. And though righteousness flows from God alone, still we shall not attain the full manifestation of it anywhere else than in the flesh of Christ, for in it was accomplished the redemption of man, in it a sacrifice was offered to atone for sins and an obedience yielded to God, to reconcile him to us. It was also filled with the sanctification of the Spirit, and at length, having vanquished death, it was received into the heavenly glory. It follows, therefore, that all the parts of life have been placed in it, that no man may have reason to complain that he is deprived of life, as if it were placed in concealment, or at a distance.

GUILLAUME FAREL (1489–1565)

French Reformer, responsible for Calvin's ministerial appointment in Geneva. Calvin, as well as others, recognized Farel for his zeal.

10

The Spirit and Faith[1]

Without the Spirit man is incapable of faith

Paul calls faith itself, which the Spirit gives us but which we do not have by nature, "the spirit of faith" (2 Cor. 4:13). He therefore prays that in the Thessalonians "God...may fulfill with power all his good pleasure...and work of faith" (2 Thess. 1:11). Here Paul calls faith "the work of God" and, instead of distinguishing it by an adjective, appropriately calls it "good pleasure." Thus he denies that man himself initiates faith, and not satisfied with this, he adds that it is a manifestation of God's power. In the letter to the Corinthians he states that faith does not depend on men's wisdom but is founded on the might of the Spirit (1 Cor. 2:4–5). He is speaking, indeed, of outward miracles, but because the wicked, being blind, cannot see these, he includes also that inner seal that he mentions elsewhere (Eph. 1:13; 4:30). And God, to show forth his liberality more fully in such a glorious gift, does not bestow it on all indiscriminately, but by a singular privilege gives it to whom he will. We have above cited testimonies of this. Augustine, the faithful interpreter of them, exclaims: "Our Savior, to teach us that belief comes as a gift and not from merit, says: 'No one comes to me, unless my Father...

---

1. Institutes 3.2.35–36.

draw him' (John 6:44), and '...it be granted him by my Father' (John 6:65). It is strange that two hear: one despises, the other rises up! Let him who despises impute it to himself; let him who rises up not arrogate it to himself."

In another passage Augustine says: "Why is it given to one and not to another? I am not ashamed to say: 'This is the depth of the cross.' Out of some depth or other of God's judgments, which we cannot fathom...comes forth all that we can do.... I see what I can do; I do not see whence I can do it—except that I see this far: that...it is of God. But why one and not the other? This means much to me. It is an abyss, the depth of the cross. I can exclaim in wonder; I cannot demonstrate it through disputation." To sum up: Christ, when he illumines us into faith by the power of his Spirit, at the same time so engrafts us into his body that we become partakers of every good.

Faith as a matter of the heart
It now remains to pour into the heart itself what the mind has absorbed. For the Word of God is not received by faith if it flits about in the top of the brain, but when it takes root in the depth of the heart that it may be an invincible defense to withstand and drive off all the stratagems of temptation. But if it is true that the mind's real understanding is illumination by the Spirit of God, then in such confirmation of the heart his power is much more clearly manifested, to the extent that the heart's distrust is greater than the mind's blindness. It is harder for the heart to be furnished with assurance than for the mind to be endowed with thought.

The Spirit accordingly serves as a seal, to seal up in our hearts those very promises the certainty of which it has previously impressed on our minds, and takes the place of a guarantee to confirm and establish them. After "you believed," the apostle declares, "you were sealed with the Holy Spirit of promise, who is the guarantee of our inheritance" (Eph. 1:13–14). Do you see how Paul teaches that the hearts of believers have, so to speak, been sealed with the Spirit; how, for this reason, Paul calls him the "Spirit of promise," because he makes firm the gospel among us? In like manner, he says in the letter to the Corinthians, "He who ... has anointed us, is God; who has also sealed us, and given the guarantee of the Spirit in our hearts" (2 Cor. 1:21–22). And, in another passage, when Paul speaks of confidence and boldness of hope, he lays as its foundation the guarantee of the Spirit (2 Cor. 5:5).

THEODORE BEZA (1519–1605)

French Reformer, became Calvin's successor in
Geneva, as well as Calvin's first biographer. He
was quite the "renaissance man," being an accomplished poet, linguist, exegete, theologian, speaker,
pastor, educator, and leader in religious and political affairs.

11

Faith's Boldness and Confidence[1]

"Through whom we have boldness and access with confidence, through the faith of him."
—Ephesians 3:12

Through whom we have boldness. The honor of reconciling the Father to the whole world must be given to Christ. From the effects of this grace its excellence is demonstrated, for *faith* that is possessed by Gentiles in common with Jews admits them into the presence of God. When the words *through Christ* and *by the faith of him* are used by Paul in connection with the name of God, there is always an implied contrast, which shuts up every other approach—which excludes every other method of obtaining divine fellowship. Most important and valuable instruction is here conveyed. The true nature and power of faith, and the confidence that is necessary for calling on God, are beautifully expressed. That the consequences of faith, and the duties that it performs, should be the subject of much controversy between us and the papists is not surprising. They do not properly understand the meaning of the word *faith*, which they

---

1. *Commentary* on Ephesians 3:12.

might learn from this passage if they were not blinded by prejudice.

First, Paul denominates it *the faith of Christ*, by which he intimates that everything that faith ought to contemplate is exhibited to us in Christ. Hence it follows that an empty and confused knowledge of Christ must not be mistaken for faith, but that knowledge that is directed to Christ, in order to seek God in Christ; and this can only be done when the power and offices of Christ are understood. *Faith* produces *confidence*, which again, in its turn, produces *boldness.* There are three stages in our progress. First, we believe the promises of God; next, by relying on them, we obtain that *confidence*, which is accompanied by holiness and peace of mind; and last of all comes *boldness*, which enables us to banish fear and to come with firmness and steadiness into the presence of God.

To separate *faith* from *confidence* would be an attempt to take away heat and light from the sun. I acknowledge, indeed, that in proportion to the measure of faith, confidence is small in some and greater in others, but faith will never be found unaccompanied by these effects or fruits. A trembling, hesitating, doubting conscience will always be a sure evidence of unbelief, but a firm, steady faith will prove to be invincible against the gates of hell. To trust in Christ as Mediator and to entertain a firm conviction of our heavenly Father's love—to venture boldly to promise to ourselves eternal life, and not to tremble at death or hell—is, to use a common phrase, a holy presumption.

Observe the expression *access with confidence.* Wicked men seek rest in forgetfulness of God and are never at ease but when they remove to the greatest possible distance from God. His own children differ from them in this respect, that they "have peace with God" (Rom. 5:1) and approach to him with cheerfulness and delight. We infer, likewise, from this passage that, in order to call on God in a proper manner, *confidence* is necessary and thus becomes the key that opens to us the gate of heaven. Those who doubt and hesitate will never be heard. "Let him ask in faith," says James, "nothing wavering: for he that wavereth is like a wave of the sea driven with the wind and tossed. For let not that man think that he shall receive anything of the Lord" (James 1:6–7).

PIERRE VIRET (1511–1571)

Swiss Reformer, ministered in Lausanne. He was a close friend and frequent correspondent of Calvin. Known for his missionary efforts in France, and was considered one of the most popular French-speaking preachers of his day.

12

Faith Struggling against Temptation[1]

Still, someone will say: "Believers experience something far different. In recognizing the grace of God
toward themselves they are not only tried by disquiet,
which often comes upon them, but they are repeatedly shaken by gravest terrors. For so violent are the
temptations that trouble their minds as not to seem
quite compatible with that certainty of faith." Accordingly, we shall have to solve this difficulty if we wish
the above-stated doctrine to stand. Surely, while we
teach that faith ought to be certain and assured, we
cannot imagine any certainty that is not tinged with
doubt, or any assurance that is not assailed by some
anxiety. On the other hand, we say that believers are
in perpetual conflict with their own unbelief. Far,
indeed, are we from putting their consciences in any
peaceful repose, undisturbed by any tumult at all....

And yet — and this is something marvelous —
amidst all these assaults, faith sustains the hearts of
the godly and truly in its effect resembles a palm tree
(cf. Ps. 92:12): for it strives against every burden and
raises itself upward. So David, even when he might
have seemed overwhelmed, in rebuking himself did
not cease to rise up to God. He who, struggling
with his own weakness, presses toward faith in his

---

1. Institutes 3.2.17–19.

moments of anxiety is already in large part victorious. Thus we may infer from this statement and ones like it: "Wait for Jehovah, be strong; he will strengthen our heart. Wait for Jehovah!" (Ps. 27:14)....

In order to understand this, it is necessary to return to that division of flesh and spirit that we have mentioned elsewhere. It most clearly reveals itself at this point. Therefore the godly heart feels in itself a division because it is partly imbued with sweetness from its recognition of the divine goodness, partly grieves in bitterness from an awareness of its calamity; partly rests on the promise of the gospel, partly trembles at the evidence of its own iniquity; partly rejoices at the expectation of life, partly shudders at death. This variation arises from imperfection of faith, since in the course of the present life it never goes so well with us that we are wholly cured of the disease of unbelief and entirely filled and possessed by faith. Hence arise those conflicts, when unbelief, which reposes in the remains of the flesh, rises up to attack the faith that has been inwardly conceived.

But if in the believing mind certainty is mixed with doubt, do we not always come back to this, that faith does not rest in a certain and clear knowledge, but only in an obscure and confused knowledge of the divine will toward us? Not at all. For even if we are distracted by various thoughts, we are not on that account completely divorced from faith. Nor if we are troubled on all sides by the agitation of unbelief are we for that reason immersed in its abyss. If we are struck, we are not for that reason cast down from our position. For the end of the conflict is always this:

that faith ultimately triumphs over those difficulties that besiege and seem to imperil it.

To sum up: When first even the least drop of faith is instilled in our minds, we begin to contemplate God's face, peaceful and calm and gracious toward us. We see him afar off, but so clearly as to know we are not at all deceived. Then, the more we advance as we ought continually to advance, with steady progress, as it were, the nearer and thus surer sight of him we obtain; and by the very continuance he is made even more familiar to us. So we see that the mind, illumined by the knowledge of God, is at first wrapped up in much ignorance, which is gradually dispelled. Yet, by being ignorant of certain things, or by rather obscurely discerning what it does discern, the mind is not hindered from enjoying a clear knowledge of the divine will toward itself. For what it discerns comprises the first and principal parts in faith. It is like a man who, shut up in a prison into which the sun's rays shine obliquely and half obscured through a rather narrow window, is indeed deprived of the full sight of the sun. Yet his eyes dwell on its steadfast brightness, and he receives its benefits. Thus, bound with fetters of an earthly body, however much we are shadowed on every side with great darkness, we are nevertheless illumined as much as need be for firm assurance when, to show forth his mercy, the light of God sheds even a little of its radiance.

HEINRICH BULLINGER (1504–1575)

Swiss Reformer, succeeded Zwingli in Zurich. He collaborated with Calvin and others to present a unified front for the Reformed churches. He drafted the Second Helvetic Confession, published numerous books, and wrote thousands of letters promoting the Reformed faith.

13

Justification Inseparable from Sanctification[1]

"But if, seeking to be justified in Christ, we ourselves also are found sinners, is Christ therefore
the minister of sin? By no means. For if I build
again those things which I destroyed, I make
myself a transgressor. For by the law I am dead
to the law. That I might live to God, I am cruci-
fied with Christ. Now it is no longer I that live,
but Christ liveth in me; and that I now live in the
flesh, I live by the faith of the Son of God, who
loved me, and gave himself for me."
—Galatians 2:17–20

If we have experienced such a death—that is, if
we have already been truly humbled and brought
low—Paul's next statement applies to us: "I am cru-
cified with Christ: nevertheless I live." Paul teaches
that our Lord Jesus Christ not only brings remission
of sins, but also sanctifies and renews us by the Holy
Spirit. Then (although we were previously full of
rebellion against God), we become devoted to his
service and to pleasing him.

---

1. Sermon on Galatians 2:17–20

In order to understand more clearly what Paul is teaching, we need to remember that there are two main benefits applied to us through the grace of the Lord Jesus Christ. One is remission of sins, which gives us assurance of salvation and peace of conscience; if this is our foundation, we may call God our Father. What is it that gives us the boldness to lift up our eyes to heaven and call him our Father? And what is it that gives us the boldness to proclaim that we are fellow-servants with the angels? It is the fact that our sins are no longer imputed to us, since we continually resort to the cleansing obtained for us by the sufferings and death of the Lord Jesus Christ. This is how we are justified.

God overlooks our unworthiness and accepts us because he sees the obedience of the Lord Jesus Christ, through whom all our transgressions are blotted out. This is the first benefit that comes to us directly from the Lord Jesus Christ. But there is also a second. Although by nature we are perverse and our free will (as the papists call it) is completely wild, men still believe in their own worth. This is despite the fact that they are full of malice, with twisted, sinful, and corrupt personalities. Although, I say, we are in such a condition, the Lord Jesus Christ grants us grace so that we may seek what is good and detest our sins. For as long as we remain in our sinful state, we seem to boast and revel in our fleshliness. But when once we have tasted the inestimable love of our God and known the Lord Jesus Christ, we become so affected by his Holy Spirit that we condemn evil and seek to draw nearer to God in conformity to his holy will. This is, therefore, the second benefit.

Even though we seem to be limping along the pathway, we are, nevertheless, growing daily in the knowledge of our imperfections and weaknesses. The Holy Spirit leads us in this way, and he makes it our main aim to reject what is sinful and fleshly and to seek, rather, to glorify God and truly obey him in every aspect of our lives. This, then, is the second gift that the Lord Jesus Christ bestows on us.

The two things are inseparably joined together, just as the brightness of the sun cannot be separated from its heat. The remission of our sins and our justification are inseparable from the regenerative work of the Spirit of sanctification. These two benefits are thus linked together. When we say that the sun is hot, it will most likely be shining at the same time, yet the brilliance of the sun is not the same as its heat. Likewise, when we say that we have been justified through the remission of our sins, it does not mean that Jesus Christ will then allow us to mock or despise him. No, we must be truly cleansed and learn to turn our backs on this world and even on ourselves in order to cleave to him in true obedience.

PHILIPP MELANCHTHON (1497–1560)

German Reformer, associate of Luther, and key leader among Lutherans. In spite of their doctrinal differences, Calvin maintained great admiration for and appreciative correspondence with the irenic Lutheran theologian.

14

What Is Justification?[1]

[Justification] is the main hinge on which religion
turns, so that we devote the greater attention and
care to it. For unless you first of all grasp what your
relationship to God is, and the nature of his judgment
concerning you, you have neither a foundation on
which to establish your salvation, nor one on which
to build piety toward God. But the need to know this
will better appear from the knowledge itself.

But that we may not stumble on the very thresh-
old—and this would happen if we should enter upon
a discussion of a thing unknown—first let us explain
what these expressions mean: that man is justified in
God's sight, and that he is justified by faith or works.
He is said to be justified in God's sight who is both
reckoned righteous in God's judgment and has been
accepted on account of his righteousness. Indeed, as
iniquity is abominable to God, so no sinner can find
favor in his eyes insofar as he is a sinner and so long as
he is reckoned as such. Accordingly, wherever there is
sin, there also the wrath and vengeance of God show
themselves. Now he is justified who is reckoned in the
condition not of a sinner but of a righteous man, and
for that reason he stands firm before God's judgment
seat while all sinners fall. If an innocent, accused per-

---

1. Institutes 3.11.1–2.

son be summoned before the judgment seat of a fair judge, where he will be judged according to his innocence, he is said to be "justified" before the judge. Thus, justified before God is the man who, freed from the company of sinners, has God to witness and affirm his righteousness. In the same way, therefore, he in whose life that purity and holiness will be found that deserves a testimony of righteousness before God's throne will be said to be justified by works, or else he who, by the wholeness of his works, can meet and satisfy God's judgment. On the contrary, justified by faith is he who, excluded from the righteousness of works, grasps the righteousness of Christ through faith and, clothed in it, appears in God's sight not as a sinner but as a righteous man.

Therefore, we explain justification simply as the acceptance with which God receives us into his favor as righteous men. And we say that it consists in the remission of sins and the imputation of Christ's righteousness.

15

The Means and Source of Sanctification[1]

"Sanctify them by thy truth: thy word is truth. As thou hast sent me into the world, I also have sent them into the world. And for their sakes I sanctify myself, that they also may be sanctified by the truth."

—John 17:17–19

Sanctify them by thy truth. This *sanctification* includes the kingdom of God and his righteousness—that is, when God renews us by his Spirit, and confirms in us the grace of renewal, and continues it to the end. [Jesus] asks, first, therefore, that the Father would sanctify the disciples, or, in other words, that he would consecrate them entirely to himself, and defend them as his sacred inheritance. Next, he points out the means of *sanctification*, and not without reason, for there are fanatics who indulge in much useless prattle about *sanctification* but who neglect *the truth* of God, by which he consecrates us to himself. Again, as there are others who chatter quite as foolishly about *the truth* and yet disregard *the word*, Christ expressly says that *the truth*, by which God sanctifies his sons, is not to be found any where else than in *the word*.

---

1. *Commentary* on John 17:17–19.

Thy word is truth; for *the word* here denotes the doctrine of the gospel, which the apostles had already heard from the mouth of their Master, and which they were afterwards to preach to others. In this sense Paul says that "the church has been cleansed with the washing of water by the word of life" (Eph. 5:26). True, it is God alone who *sanctifies*; but since "the gospel is the power of God to salvation to everyone that believeth" (Rom. 1:16), whoever departs from the gospel as the means must become more and more filthy and polluted.

The truth is here taken, by way of eminence, for the light of heavenly wisdom, in which God manifests himself to us, that he may conform us to his image. The outward preaching of *the word,* it is true, does not of itself accomplish this, for that preaching is wickedly profaned by the reprobate; but let us remember that Christ speaks of the elect, whom the Holy Spirit efficaciously regenerates *by the word.* Now, since the apostles were not altogether destitute of this grace, we ought to infer from Christ's words that *sanctification* is not instantly completed in us on the first day, but that we make progress in it through the whole course of our life, till at length God, having taken away from us the garment of the flesh, fills us with his righteousness.

As thou hast sent me into the world. He confirms his prayer by another argument—namely, because the calling of Christ and of the apostles is the same calling, and is common to both. "I now," he says, "appoint them to an office, which I have hitherto held by thy command; and, therefore, it is necessary that they should be furnished with the power of thy Spirit, that they may be able to sustain so weighty a charge."

And for their sakes I sanctify myself. By these words he explains more clearly from what source that *sanctification* flows, which is completed in us by the doctrine of the gospel. It is, because he consecrates himself to the Father, that his holiness might come to us. For as the blessing on the firstfruits is spread over the whole harvest, so the Spirit of God cleanses us by the holiness of Christ and makes us partakers of it. Nor is this done by imputation only, for in that respect he is said to have been *made to us righteousness*; but he is likewise said to have been *made to us sanctification* (1 Cor. 1:30), because he has, so to speak, presented us to his Father in his own person, that we may be renewed to true holiness by his Spirit. Besides, though this sanctification belongs to the whole life of Christ, yet the highest illustration of it was given in the sacrifice of his death, for then he showed himself to be the true High Priest, by consecrating the temple, the altar, all the vessels, and the people, by the power of his Spirit.

SECTION FOUR

Ecclesiological Dimensions

- *Piety through the Church*
  (chapters 16–18)

- *Piety of the Word* (chapters 19–21)

- *Piety in the Sacraments*
  (chapters 22–24)

- *Piety in the Psalter* (chapters 25–27)

16

Confessing the Church's Holiness[1]

Because [all godly men] also allege that the church is
not without basis called holy, it is fitting to examine
in what holiness it excels lest, if we are not willing to
admit a church unless it be perfect in every respect,
we leave no church at all. True, indeed, is Paul's
statement: "Christ...gave himself up for the church
that he might sanctify her; he cleansed her by the
washing of water in the word of life, that he might
present her to himself as his glorious bride, without
spot or wrinkle..." (Eph. 5:25–27). Yet it also is no
less true that the Lord is daily at work in smoothing
out wrinkles and cleansing spots. From this it follows that the church's holiness is not yet complete.
The church is holy, then, in the sense that it is daily
advancing and is not yet perfect: it makes progress
from day to day but has not yet reached its goal of
holiness, as will be explained more fully elsewhere.

The prophets prophesy that there will be a holy
Jerusalem through which "strangers shall never pass"
(Joel 3:17), and a most holy temple wherein the
unclean shall not enter (Isa. 35:8; cf. ch. 52:1). Let us
not understand this prophecy as if all the members
of the church were without blemish; but because
they zealously aspire to holiness and perfect purity,

---

1. Institutes 4.1.17.

the cleanness that they have not yet fully attained is granted them by God's kindness. And although there are oftentimes few evidences of this sort of sanctification among men, still we must hold that from the creation of the world there was no time when the Lord did not have his church, and even until the consummation of the age, there will be no time when he will not have it. For even though the whole human race has from the very beginning been corrupted and vitiated by Adam's sin, from this polluted mass, as it were, he ever sanctifies certain vessels unto honor (cf. Rom. 9:23ff.), that there may be no age that does not experience his mercy. This he has attested by sure promises such as these: "I have made a covenant with my chosen ones, I have sworn to David my servant: 'I will perpetuate your seed forever and build your throne for all generations'" (Ps. 89:3–4). Also: "The Lord has chosen Zion; he has chosen it for his habitation; this is my resting place forever..." (Ps. 132:13–14). Also: "Thus says the Lord, who gives the sun for light by day, and...the moon and stars for light by night.... If these laws fail before me,... then shall the seed of Israel fail" (Jer. 31:35–36).

17

Keeping Sunday Holy[1]

> "Keep the day of rest, to hallow it as the LORD thy God hath commanded thee. Six days shalt thou labor, and do all thy business: but the seventh day is the rest of the LORD thy God, thou shalt not do any work therein."
>
> —Deuteronomy 5:12–14

Let us realize that it is not only for coming to the sermon that the day of Sunday is instituted, but in order that we might devote all the rest of time to praising God. Indeed! For although he nurtures us every day, nevertheless we do not sufficiently meditate on the favors he bestows on us in order to magnify them. It is true that it would be a poor thing if we did not think about the benefits of God except on Sunday, but on other days, seeing that we are so occupied with our affairs, we are not as much open to serve God as on a day that is totally dedicated to this. Thus we ought to observe Sunday as if from a tower, in order that we might climb high up on it to contemplate the works of God from afar, in a way in which we are neither impeded by nor occupied with anything else, so that we might be able to extend all our senses to recognize

---

1. Sermon on Deuteronomy 5:12–14.

the benefits and favors with which he has enlarged us.
And when Sunday is able to help us practice that—
that is, to consider the works of God—then certainly
once we have meditated on his works for a long time
in order to know how to benefit from them, we will
surrender to him all the rest of time. For this medita-
tion will already have formed and polished us, [and]
we shall be induced to thank our God on Monday
and all the rest of the week. But when Sunday is spent
not only in pastimes full of vanity, but in things that
are entirely contrary to God, it seems that one has
not at all celebrated Sunday [and] that God has been
offended in many ways. Thus, when people profane
in this manner the holy order that God has instituted
to lead us to himself, why should they be astonished
if all the rest of the week is degraded?

Thus, what is necessary? Let us recognize that it is
not enough for us to come to the sermon on Sunday
in order to receive some good doctrine and to invoke
the name of God, but it is necessary to ponder these
things and to apply all our senses to understanding
better the favors that God bestows on us. And by this
means may we be molded by what costs us nothing,
[whether] on Monday or any other day of the week,
to aspire to our God. May we reduce to memory
only what we have previously known by [his] good
leisure, that our minds may be delivered from all
that hinders us and prevents us from recognizing the
works of God. Thus, that is how we ought to observe
today this matter concerning the order. We no longer
have this figure and shadow for the purpose of keeping a ceremony as rigid as it was under the bondage
of the law. Rather, its purpose is to gather us, in order

that according to our weakness we might be trained to devote ourselves better to the service of God, that we might have this day fully dedicated to him, to the end that we might be withdrawn from the world and, as we have said, that it might serve us for the rest of our life.

Moreover, we have to note that on Sunday it is not enough for each in his own way to think of God and his work, but it is essential for us to gather on that particular day in order to make a public confession of our faith. In truth, as we have said, that ought to be done every day, yet because of men's coarseness and because of their nonchalance, it is necessary to have a special day that should be totally dedicated to that end.

MARTIN BUCER (1491–1551)

German Reformer, ministered in Strasbourg, and fought ardently for a consensus among the churches of the Reformation. Calvin benefitted greatly from Bucer's understanding of the church.

18

Sharing Gifts for the Church's Good[1]

> "For as in one body we have many members, but all the members have not the same office; so we, being many, are one body in Christ, and severally members of one another. Now having gifts differing according to the grace given to us, whether prophecy, let us use it according to the analogy of faith."
>
> —Romans 12:4–6

For as in one body.... The very thing that [Paul] had previously said of limiting the wisdom of each according to the measure of faith, he now confirms by a reference to the vocation of the faithful. For we are called for this end, that we may unite together in one body, since Christ has ordained a fellowship and connection between the faithful, similar to the one that exists between the members of the human body; and as men could not of themselves come together into such an union, he himself becomes the bond of this connection. As then the case is with the human body, so it ought to be with the society of the faithful. By applying this similitude he proves how necessary it is for each to consider what is suitable to his own nature,

---

1. *Commentary* on Romans 12:4–6.

capacity, and vocation. But though this similitude has various parts, it is yet to be chiefly thus applied to our present subject—that as the members of the same body have distinct offices (and all of them are distinct, for no member possesses all powers, nor does it appropriate to itself the offices of others), so God has distributed various gifts to us, by which diversity he has determined the order that he would have to be observed among us, so that everyone is to conduct himself according to the measure of his capacity and not to thrust himself into what peculiarly belongs to others; nor is anyone to seek to have all things himself, but to be content with his lot, and willingly to abstain from usurping the offices of others. When, however, he points out in express words the communion that is between us, he at the same time intimates how much diligence there ought to be in all, so that they may contribute to the common good of the body according to the faculties they possess.

Having gifts.... Paul speaks now not simply of cherishing among ourselves brotherly love, but [he] commends humility, which is the best moderator of our whole life. Everyone desires to have so much himself, so as not to need any help from others; but the bond of mutual communication is this: that no one has sufficient for himself, but is constrained to borrow from others. I admit then that the society of the godly cannot exist except when each one is content with his own measure, and imparts to others the gifts that he has received, and allows himself by turns to be assisted by the gifts of others.

But Paul especially intended to beat down the pride that he knew to be innate in men, and that no one might be dissatisfied that all things have not been bestowed on him, he reminds us that according to the wise counsel of God everyone has his own portion given to him. For it is necessary to the common benefit of the body that no one should be furnished with fullness of gifts, lest he should heedlessly despise his brethren. Here then we have the main design that the apostle had in view: that all things do not meet in all, but that the gifts of God are so distributed that each has a limited portion, and that each ought to be so attentive in imparting his own gifts to the edification of the church, that no one, by leaving his own function, may trespass on that of another. By this most beautiful order and, as it were, symmetry, is the safety of the church indeed preserved—that is, when everyone imparts to all in common what he has received from the Lord, in such a way as not to impede others. He who inverts this order fights with God, by whose ordinance it is appointed. For the difference of gifts proceeds not from the will of man, but because it has pleased the Lord to distribute his grace in this manner.

ROBERT STEPHENS (1503–1559)

French typographer, converted from Catholicism, and moved from Paris to Geneva. He befriended Calvin and printed books for him. He was known for printing Bibles, and was the first to use chapter and verse divisions.

19

True Knowledge by the Word[1]

The Word of God as Holy Scripture

Whether God became known to the patriarchs through oracles and visions or by the work and ministry of men, he put into their minds what they should then hand down to their posterity. At any rate, there is no doubt that firm certainty of doctrine was engraved in their hearts, so that they were convinced and understood that what they had learned proceeded from God. For by his Word, God rendered faith unambiguous forever, a faith that should be superior to all opinion.

Finally, in order that truth might abide forever in the world with a continuing succession of teaching and survive through all ages, the same oracles he had given to the patriarchs it was his pleasure to have recorded, as it were, on public tablets. With this intent the law was published, and the prophets afterward added as its interpreters. For even though the use of the law was manifold, as will be seen more clearly in its place, it was especially committed to Moses and all the prophets to teach the way of reconciliation between God and men, whence also Paul calls "Christ the end of the law" (Rom. 10:4).

---

1. Institutes 1.6.2–3.

Yet I repeat once more: besides the specific doctrine of faith and repentance that sets forth Christ as
Mediator, Scripture adorns with unmistakable marks
and tokens the one true God, in that he has created
and governs the universe, in order that he may not
be mixed up with the throng of false gods. Therefore,
however fitting it may be for man seriously to turn his
eyes to contemplate God's works, since he has been
placed in this most glorious theater to be a specta-
tor of them, it is fitting that he prick up his ears to
the Word, the better to profit. And it is therefore no
wonder that those who were born in darkness become
more and more hardened in their insensibility. For
there are very few who, to contain themselves within
bounds, apply themselves teachably to God's Word,
but they rather exult in their own vanity.

Now, in order that true religion may shine on us,
we ought to hold that it must take its beginning from
heavenly doctrine and that no one can get even the
slightest taste of right and sound doctrine unless he
be a pupil of Scripture. Hence, there also emerges
the beginning of true understanding when we rever-
ently embrace what it pleases God there to witness
of himself. But not only faith, perfect and in every
way complete, but all right knowledge of God is born
of obedience. And surely in this respect God has, by
his singular providence, taken thought for mortals
through all ages.

Without Scripture we fall into error
Suppose we ponder how slippery is the fall of the
human mind into forgetfulness of God, how great the

tendency to every kind of error, how great the lust to fashion constantly new and artificial religions. Then we may perceive how necessary was such written proof of the heavenly doctrine, that it should neither perish through forgetfulness nor vanish through error nor be corrupted by the audacity of men. It is therefore clear that God has provided the assistance of the Word for the sake of all those to whom he has been pleased to give useful instruction, because he foresaw that his likeness imprinted on the most beautiful form of the universe would be insufficiently effective.

Hence, we must strive onward by this straight path if we seriously aspire to the pure contemplation of God. We must come, I say, to the Word, where God is truly and vividly described to us from his works, while these very works are appraised not by our depraved judgment but by the rule of eternal truth. If we turn aside from the Word, as I have just now said, though we may strive with strenuous haste, yet, since we have got off the track, we shall never reach the goal. For we should so reason that the splendor of the divine countenance, which even the apostle calls "unapproachable" (1 Tim. 6:16), is for us like an inexplicable labyrinth unless we are conducted into it by the thread of the Word; so that it is better to limp along this path than to dash with all speed outside it. David very often, therefore, teaching that we ought to banish superstitions from the earth so that pure religion may flourish, represented God as regnant (Ps. 93:1; 96:10; 97:1; 99:1; and the like). Now he means by the word "regnant" not the power with which he is endowed, and which he exercises in governing the whole of nature, but the doctrine by which he asserts his lawful sovereignty. For errors can never be uprooted from human hearts until true knowledge of God is planted therein.

20

True Education through Preaching[1]

Paul writes that Christ, "that he might fill all things," appointed some to be "apostles, some prophets, some evangelists, some pastors and teachers, for the equipment of the saints, for the work of the ministry, for the building up of the body of Christ, until we all reach the unity of the faith and of the knowledge of the Son of God, to perfect manhood, to the measure of the fully mature age of Christ" (Eph. 4:10–13). We see how God, who could in a moment perfect his own, nevertheless desires them to grow up into manhood solely under the education of the church. We see the way set for it: the preaching of the heavenly doctrine has been enjoined on the pastors. We see that all are brought under the same regulation, that with a gentle and teachable spirit they may allow themselves to be governed by teachers appointed to this function. Isaiah had long before distinguished Christ's kingdom by this mark: "My spirit that is upon you, and my words that I have put in your mouth, shall never depart out of your mouth, or out of the mouth of your children, or ... of your children's children" (Isa. 59:21). From this it follows that all those who spurn the spiritual food, divinely extended to them through the hand of the church, deserve to

---

1. Institutes 4.1.5.

perish in famine and hunger. God breathes faith into us only by the instrument of his gospel, as Paul points out that "faith comes from hearing" (Rom. 10:17). Likewise, the power to save rests with God (Rom. 1:16); but, as Paul again testifies, he displays and unfolds it in the preaching of the gospel.

By this plan he willed of old that holy assemblies be held at the sanctuary, in order that the doctrine taught by the mouth of the priest might foster agreement in faith. The temple is called God's "resting place" (Ps. 132:14); the sanctuary, his "dwelling" (Isa. 57:15), where he is said to sit among the cherubim (Ps. 80:1). Glorious titles, they are used solely to bring esteem, love, reverence, and dignity to the ministry of the heavenly doctrine. Otherwise, the appearance of a mortal and despised man would much detract from them. To make us aware, then, that an inestimable treasure is given us in earthen vessels (2 Cor. 4:7), God himself appears in our midst, and, as Author of this order, would have men recognize him as present in his institution.

Accordingly, after he forbade his people to devote themselves to auguries, divinations, magic arts, necromancy, and other superstitions (Deut. 18:10–11; Lev. 19:31), he added that he would give what ought to suffice for all: that they should never be destitute of prophets (cf. Deut. 18:15). But as he did not entrust the ancient folk to angels but raised up teachers from the earth truly to perform the angelic office, so also today it is his will to teach us through human means. As he was of old not content with the law alone, but added priests as interpreters from whose lips the people might ask its true meaning (cf. Mal. 2:7), so today he not only desires us to be attentive to its reading, but also appoints instructors to help us by their effort. This is doubly useful. On the one hand, he proves our obedience by a very good test when we hear his ministers speaking, just as if he himself spoke. On the other, he also provides for our weakness in that he prefers to address us in human fashion through interpreters in order to draw us to himself, rather than to thunder at us and drive us away. Indeed, from the dread with which God's majesty justly overwhelms them, all the pious truly feel how much this familiar sort of teaching is needed.

Calvin preaching his farewell sermon
in expectation of banishment

21

True Completeness through the Word[1]

"The whole Scripture is given by inspiration of God, and is profitable to teach, to improve, to correct, to instruct in righteousness, that the man of God may be perfect, being made ready to every good work."

—2 Timothy 3:16–17

We see, therefore, that St. Paul means to show that we must make the Word of God serve for this purpose: that we may model our lives according to it and walk uprightly. So he ends by saying, "that the man of God may be complete, thoroughly equipped for every good work" (v. 17). This matter of instruction in righteousness is all the more appropriate in order to show plainly that all the inventions of men are to be excluded. For otherwise everyone would serve God according to his own ideas, but that would make God subject to our whims; or again, if we thought up good works to suit ourselves, they would not be acceptable to God.

St. Paul, seeing such impudence and boldness in men that they always want to take their own works

---

1. Sermon on 2 Timothy 3:16–17.

into account and are not content to keep within the limits and bounds that God has set for them, points out the disease here, so that it might more easily be healed. He tells us that if we have the Word of God in our hearts, there will be a completeness about us, for we shall lack nothing but shall be "thoroughly equipped for every good work." When he says that we shall be "complete" (or "perfect"), he means that we shall be like a body that is in every respect well-formed, well-proportioned, and attractive, with no parts missing. The word he uses conveys this sense of lacking nothing. Let us, therefore, note that we are by nature absolutely nothing at all, but God restores his image in us by means of his Word, and this is how we come to the completeness of which Paul speaks....

It is said here that we shall be equipped for every good work, if we profit by Holy Scripture.... Therefore, let us stop consciously and willingly deceiving ourselves, considering that we shall find in Holy Scripture a full sufficiency of all that is required for our completeness and for all good works, and that God excludes anything that might be added to what is prescribed in it, and shows that such things will not be taken into account, nor are they to be laid down as things that are acceptable to him. Men, therefore, draw up all their regulations in vain; it will only serve to double their condemnation.

Someone might ask, "If the law and the prophets are so complete, what purpose does the gospel serve? It would seem at this rate that we do not even need Paul's teaching." This can easily be answered. The gospel was not given to men to add anything to either the law or the prophets. Let us read every page of the New Testament—we shall not find one syllable added to either the law or the prophets; it only sets forth more plainly what was taught in them. It is true that God has been more gracious to us than to the Old Testament saints who lived before the coming of the Lord Jesus Christ, in that matters are more clearly set forth for us, but nothing is added. So, then, when St. Paul declares that we shall find completeness and perfect righteousness in the law and the prophets, it does not in any way detract from the gospel, for all of Holy Scripture is in agreement, both Old and New Testaments. The doctrine that was contained in the law has been expounded to us so well by the apostles who came after Jesus Christ that we cannot say, "We must do this or that"—other than what was commanded from the very beginning. Indeed, God has made so many things clear to us and has given so many reasons [why we should believe it], that we would have to be perverse indeed not to be convinced of these truths by their very familiarity.

Therefore, if we are to profit from Holy Scripture, we must apply ourselves to study holiness of life, knowing that God will not be served according to our own ideas, but that he has given us a sure and sufficient rule by which we should regulate our lives, and one with which we cannot find fault. Let us, then, direct our every thought and the affections of our hearts towards what is contained in Holy Scripture. Then the heavenly Judge will be pleased with us. We must pay all the more attention to these things, because we see that our good God draws near to us and has set out his will so plainly for us that we have no excuse, but must cling fast to him alone.

PETER MARTYR VERMIGLI (1499–1562)

Italian Reformer, fled Italy and accepted appoint-
ments at Oxford, Strasbourg, and Zurich. His views
on the Sacraments stood between the Lutheran and
Zwinglian positions, stressing the efficacy of the
Spirit. Calvin thought much of Vermigli, concurred
with his stance on the Sacraments, and even desired
for him to lead the Italian church in Geneva.

22

The Spirit in the Sacraments[1]

As to the confirmation and increase of faith, I should like my readers to be reminded that I assign this particular ministry to the sacraments. Not that I suppose there is some secret force or other perpetually seated in them by which they are able to promote or confirm faith by themselves. Rather, I consider that they have been instituted by the Lord to the end that they may serve to establish and increase faith.

But the sacraments properly fulfill their office only when the Spirit, that inward teacher, comes to them, by whose power alone hearts are penetrated and affections moved and our souls opened for the sacraments to enter in. If the Spirit be lacking, the sacraments can accomplish nothing more in our minds than the splendor of the sun shining on blind eyes, or a voice sounding in deaf ears. Therefore, I make such a division between Spirit and sacraments that the power to act rests with the former, and the ministry alone is left to the latter—a ministry empty and trifling, apart from the action of the Spirit, but charged with great effect when the Spirit works within and manifests his power.

Now it is clear in what way, according to this opinion, the godly mind is strengthened in faith

---

1. Institutes 4.14.9–10.

through the sacraments. That is, just as the eyes see by the brightness of the sun, or the ears hear by the sound of a voice, so the eyes would not be affected by any light unless they were endowed with a sharpness of vision capable of being illumined of themselves; and the ears would never be struck by any noise, unless they were created and fitted for hearing. But suppose it is true (something that ought at once to be clear among us) that what sight does in our eyes for seeing light, and what hearing does in our ears for perceiving a voice, are analogous to the work of the Holy Spirit in our hearts, which is to conceive, sustain, nourish, and establish faith. Then both of these things follow: the sacraments profit not a whit without the power of the Holy Spirit, and nothing prevents them from strengthening and enlarging faith in hearts already taught by that Schoolmaster. There is only this difference: that our ears and eyes have naturally received the faculty of hearing and seeing; but Christ does the same thing in our hearts by special grace beyond the measure of nature....

That the Word may not beat your ears in vain, and that the sacraments may not strike your eyes in vain, the Spirit shows us that in them it is God speaking to us, softening the stubbornness of our heart, and composing it to the obedience that it owes the Word of the Lord. Finally, the Spirit transmits those outward words and sacraments from our ears to our soul.

Therefore, Word and sacraments confirm our faith when they set before our eyes the good will of our Heavenly Father toward us, by the knowledge of whom the whole firmness of our faith stands fast and increases in strength. The Spirit confirms it when, by engraving this confirmation in our minds, he makes it effective. Meanwhile, the Father of Lights (cf. James 1:17) cannot be hindered from illumining our minds with a sort of intermediate brilliance through the sacraments, just as he illumines our bodily eyes by the rays of the sun.

JOHN KNOX (ca. 1514–1572)

Scottish Reformer, ministered to the English-speaking church in Geneva. He maintained correspondence with Calvin, and sought to bring Genevan reforms back to Scotland.

23

━━━►■◄(•)►■◄━━━

Dying to Become New Creatures[1]

"Know ye not, that we all, who have been baptized into Jesus Christ, have been baptized into
his death? We have then been buried with him
through baptism unto death, that as Christ was
raised from the dead by the glory of the Father, so
we also should walk in newness of life."
                                        —Romans 6:3–4

Know ye not.... What Paul intimated in the last
verse—that Christ destroys sin in his people—he
proves here by mentioning the effect of baptism, by
which we are initiated into his faith. For it is beyond
any question that we put on Christ in baptism, and
that we are baptized for this end—that we may be one
with him. But Paul takes up another principle—that
we are then really united to the body of Christ when
his death brings forth in us its fruit; yea, he teaches us
that this fellowship as to death is what is to be mainly
regarded in baptism, for [it is] not washing alone
[that] is set forth in it, but also the putting to death
and the dying of the old man. It is hence evident that
when we become partakers of the grace of Christ,
immediately the efficacy of his death appears. But the

---

1. *Commentary* on Romans 6:3–4.

benefit of this fellowship as to the death of Christ is described in what follows.

We have then been buried with him.... He now begins to indicate the object of our having been baptized into the death of Christ, though he does not yet completely unfold it; and the object is that we, being dead to ourselves, may become new creatures. He rightly makes a transition from a fellowship in death to a fellowship in life, for these two things are connected together by an indissoluble knot—that the old man is destroyed by the death of Christ, and that his resurrection brings righteousness and renders us new creatures. And surely, since Christ has been given to us for life, to what purpose is it that we die with him except that we may rise to a better life? And hence for no other reason does he slay what is mortal in us, but that he may give us life again.

Let us know that the apostle does not simply exhort us to imitate Christ, as though he had said that the death of Christ is a pattern that all Christians are to follow. For no doubt he ascends higher, since he announces a doctrine with which he connects, as it is evident, an exhortation; and his doctrine is this—that the death of Christ is efficacious to destroy and demolish the depravity of our flesh, and his resurrection, to effect the renovation of a better nature, and that by baptism we are admitted into a participation of this grace. This foundation being laid, Christians may very suitably be exhorted to strive to respond to their calling.

Further, it is not to the point to say that this power is not apparent in all the baptized, for Paul, according to his usual manner, where he speaks of the faithful, connects the reality and the effect with the outward sign. For we know that whatever the Lord offers by the visible symbol is confirmed and ratified by their faith. In short, he teaches what is the real character of baptism when rightly received. So he testifies to the Galatians that all who have been baptized into Christ have put on Christ (Gal. 3:27). Thus indeed must we speak, as long as the institution of the Lord and the faith of the godly unite together, for we never have naked and empty symbols, except when our ingratitude and wickedness hinder the working of divine beneficence.

Calvin refusing the Lord's Supper
to the Libertines
in St. Peter's Cathedral, Geneva

24

Being Members of Christ[1]

Let us take the side of our Lord Jesus Christ, if we wish to experience to our salvation the profit and the fulfillment of what is here narrated by St. Luke [in Acts 2:1–4]: namely, not only may God speak to our ears, and may his doctrine pierce our hearts, may we be inflamed, may we be remade and renewed, in such a way that the corruptions of this world may be put down, and, as we wish to be owned and acknowledged as his people, may we be able to claim in truth our God in the name of our Lord Jesus Christ, to whom we are joined in order that he may unite us in perfection to God his Father. That is also why this Holy Table is now prepared for us.

For, as I have already said, we cannot communicate any grace from the Holy Spirit without being members of our Lord Jesus Christ. How can we arrive at that condition unless he presents himself to us and he lives with us in such a manner that everything that is his belongs to us, and we enjoy the benefits that have been given to him in our name? It is said in the eleventh chapter of Isaiah that the Spirit of God has rested upon him, but not for any necessity he had of it, nor for his private use; it was for the profit of all of his body—that is to say, of all of the

---

1. Sermon on Acts 2:1–4.

church. So then, let us recognize, when now the Supper is offered to us, that our Lord Jesus wishes that we might find all our good in him; he draws near to us through his goodness.

It is true that he does not leave his heavenly glory; he need not descend here below (as the papists imagine) to communicate to us his body and his blood. But although we are far away from him, yet he does not cease to feed us with his body and his blood. Also we shall not cease to be united to him, in entire perfection—indeed, as much as it will be needed. That is why I call that "perfection," although he comes to us little by little. For though that may be, we shall not cease to be joined to him. Indeed, let us recognize that he did not wish to disappoint us when he declared that he is our Head and that we are his members, and that, if we let ourselves be governed by him, we shall experience that he will be our good and sure Guide, and that the power of his Holy Spirit is infinite in order to sustain us.

In the first place, then, when we come to this holy table, let us recognize that it is a secret that surpasses all our senses, and yet we must here give place to faith. Let us know that what cannot be conceived of by men is accomplished, nevertheless, by the secret and invisible grace of the Holy Spirit, for this is how we are made partakers of the body and of the blood of Jesus Christ.

25

Identifying with David[1]

The varied and resplendent riches that are contained in this treasury [of the Psalms] it is no easy matter to express in words; so much so, that I well know that whatever I shall be able to say will be far from approaching the excellence of the subject.... I have been accustomed to call this book, I think not inappropriately, "An Anatomy of all the Parts of the Soul," for there is not an emotion of which anyone can be conscious that is not here represented in a mirror. Or rather, the Holy Spirit has here drawn to the life all the griefs, sorrows, fears, doubts, hopes, cares, perplexities—in short, all the distracting emotions with which the minds of men are wont to be agitated.

Although the Psalms are replete with all the precepts that serve to frame our life to every part of holiness, piety, and righteousness, yet they will principally teach and train us to bear the cross; and the bearing of the cross is a genuine proof of our obedience, since by doing this we renounce the guidance of our own affections, and submit ourselves entirely to God, leaving him to govern us, and to dispose of our life according to his will, so that the afflictions that are the bitterest and most severe to our nature

---

1. Preface to *Commentary* on the Psalms, xxxvi–xxxvii, xxxix–xli.

become sweet to us, because they proceed from him. In one word, not only will we here find general commendations of the goodness of God, which may teach men to repose themselves in him alone and to seek all their happiness solely in him, and which are intended to teach true believers with their whole hearts confidently to look to him for help in all their necessities; but we will also find that the free remission of sins, which alone reconciles God towards us and procures for us settled peace with him, is so set forth and magnified as that here there is nothing wanting that relates to the knowledge of eternal salvation.

Now, if my readers derive any fruit and advantage from the labor that I have bestowed in writing these commentaries, I would have them to understand that the small measure of experience that I have had by the conflicts with which the Lord has exercised me has in no ordinary degree assisted me, not only in applying to present use whatever instruction could be gathered from these divine compositions, but also in more easily comprehending the design of each of the writers. And since David holds the principal place among them, it has greatly aided me in understanding more fully the complaints made by him of the internal afflictions that the church had to sustain through those who gave themselves out to be her members, that I had suffered the same or similar things from the domestic enemies of the church. For although I follow David at a great distance, and come far short of equaling him—or rather, although in aspiring slowly and with great difficulty to attain to the many virtues in which he excelled, I still feel myself tarnished with the contrary vices—yet if I have any things in common with him, I have no hesitation in comparing myself with him. In reading the instances of his faith, patience, fervor, zeal, and integrity, it has, as it ought, drawn from me unnumbered groans and sighs, that I am so far from approaching them; but it has, notwithstanding, been of very great advantage to me to behold in him as in a mirror, both the commencement of my calling, and the continued course of my function; so that I know the more assuredly that whatever that most illustrious king and prophet suffered was exhibited to me by God as an example for imitation.

My condition, no doubt, is much inferior to his, and it is unnecessary for me to stay to show this. But as he was taken from the sheepfold and elevated to the rank of supreme authority, so God having taken me from my originally obscure and humble condition has reckoned me worthy of being invested with the honorable office of a preacher and minister of the gospel. When I was as yet a very little boy, my father had destined me for the study of theology. But afterwards, when he considered that the legal profession commonly raised those who followed it to wealth, this prospect induced him suddenly to change his purpose. Thus it came to pass that I was withdrawn from the study of philosophy and was put to the study of law. To this pursuit I endeavored faithfully to apply myself, in obedience to the will of my father; but God, by the secret guidance of his providence, at length gave a different direction to my course. And first, since I was too obstinately devoted to the superstitions of popery to be easily extricated from so profound an abyss of mire, God by a sudden conversion subdued and brought my mind to a teachable frame, which was more hardened in such matters than might have been expected from one at my early period of life. Having thus received some taste and knowledge of true godliness, I was immediately inflamed with so intense a desire to make progress there, that although I did not altogether leave off other studies, I yet pursued them with less ardor.

26

Holiness Essential for Access to God[1]

"O Jehovah, who shall dwell in thy tabernacle?
Who shall rest in the mountain of thy holiness?"
—Psalm 15:1

David, without stopping to speak to men, addresses
himself to God, which he considers the better course;
and he intimates that if men assume the title of the
people of God without being so in deed and in truth,
they gain nothing by their self-delusion, for God
continues always like himself, and as he is faithful
himself, so will he have us to keep faith with him
in return. No doubt, he adopted Abraham freely,
but, at the same time, he stipulated with him that he
should live a holy and an upright life, and this is the
general rule of the covenant that God has, from the
beginning, made with his church. The sum is that
hypocrites, who occupy a place in the temple of God,
in vain pretend to be his people, for he acknowledges
none as such but those who follow after justice and
uprightness during the whole course of their life.
David saw the temple crowded with a great multitude of men who all made a profession of the same

---

1. *Commentary* on Psalm 15:1.

religion and presented themselves before God as to the outward ceremony; and, therefore, assuming the person of one wondering at the spectacle, he directs his discourse to God, who, in such a confusion and medley of characters, could easily distinguish his own people from strangers.

There is a threefold use of this doctrine. In the first place, if we really wish to be reckoned among the number of the children of God, the Holy Ghost teaches us that we must show ourselves to be such by a holy and an upright life. For it is not enough to serve God by outward ceremonies, unless we also live uprightly, and without doing wrong to our neighbors.

In the second place, since we too often see the church of God defaced by much impurity, to prevent us from stumbling at what appears so offensive, a distinction is made between those who are permanent citizens of the church and strangers who are mingled among them only for a time. This is undoubtedly a warning highly necessary, in order that when the temple of God happens to be tainted by many impurities, we may not contract such disgust and chagrin as will make us withdraw from it. By impurities I understand the vices of a corrupt and polluted life. Provided religion continue pure as to doctrine and worship, we must not be so much stumbled at the faults and sins that men commit, as on that account to rend the unity of the church. Yet the experience of all ages teaches us how dangerous a temptation it is when we behold the church of God, which ought to be free from all polluting stains and to shine in uncorrupted purity, cherishing in her bosom many ungodly hypocrites or wicked persons.... Christ, in Matthew 25:32, justly claims it as his own peculiar office to separate the sheep from the goats and thereby admonishes us that we must bear with the evils that it is not in our power to correct, until all things become ripe and the proper season of purging the church arrive. At the same time, the faithful are here enjoined, each in his own sphere, to use their endeavors that the church of God may be purified from the corruptions that still exist within her.

And this is the third use that we should make of this doctrine. God's sacred barn-floor will not be perfectly cleansed before the last day, when Christ at his coming will cast out the chaff; but he has already begun to do this by the doctrine of his gospel, which on this account he terms a fan. We must, therefore, by no means be indifferent about this matter; on the contrary, we ought rather to exert ourselves in good earnest, that all who profess themselves Christians may lead a holy and an unspotted life. But above all, what God here declares with respect to all the unrighteous should be deeply imprinted on our memory: namely, that he prohibits them from coming to his sanctuary and condemns their impious presumption in irreverently thrusting themselves into the society of the godly. David makes mention of *the tabernacle,* because the temple was not yet built. The meaning of his discourse, to express it in a few words, is this: that those only have access to God who are his genuine servants and who live a holy life.

AUGUSTIN MARLORAT (1506–1562)

French Reformer, ministered at Rouen, and martyred like so many Huguenots. This friend of Calvin was known for his expositions of the New Testament and his contribution to the Genevan Psalter.

27

Hoping in God despite
Discouragement[1]

"O my soul! Why art thou cast down? And why
art thou disquieted within me? Wait thou upon
God: for I shall yet praise him for the helps [or
salvations] of his countenance."

—Psalm 42:5

O my soul! Why art thou cast down? From this it appears
that David contended strongly against his sorrow, lest
he should yield to temptation. But what we ought
chiefly to observe is that he had experienced a strong
and bitter contest before he obtained the victory over
it; or we might rather say, that he was not delivered
from it after one alarming assault but was often called
on to enter into new scenes of conflict. It need not
excite our wonder that he was so much disquieted
and cast down, since he could not discern any sign of
the divine favor towards him.

But David here represents himself as if he formed
two opposing parties. Insofar as in the exercise of
faith he relied on the promises of God, being armed
with the Spirit of invincible fortitude, he set himself,
in opposition to the affections of his flesh, to restrain

---

1. *Commentary* on Psalm 42:5.

and subdue them; and, at the same time, he rebuked his own cowardice and imbecility of heart. Moreover, although he carried on war against the devil and the world, yet he does not enter into open and direct conflict with them but rather regards himself as the enemy against whom he desires chiefly to contend. And doubtless the best way to overcome Satan is not to go out of ourselves but to maintain an internal conflict against the desires of our own hearts.

It ought, however, to be observed that David confesses that his soul was cast down within him. For when our infirmities rise up in vast array and, like the waves of the sea, are ready to overwhelm us, our faith seems to us to fail, and, in consequence, we are so overcome by mere fear that we lack courage and are afraid to enter into the conflict. Whenever, therefore, such a state of indifference and faintheartedness shall seize upon us, let us remember that to govern and subdue the desires of their hearts, and especially to contend against the feelings of distrust that are natural to all, is a conflict to which the godly are not infrequently called.

But here there are two evils specified, which, however apparently different, yet assail our hearts at the same time: the one is *discouragement* and the other *disquietude.* When we are quite downcast, we are not free of a feeling of disquietude, which leads us to murmur and complain. The remedy to both of them is here added: *hope in God*, which alone inspires our minds, in the first place, with confidence in the midst of the greatest troubles; and, secondly, by the exercise of patience, preserves them in peace. In what follows, David very well expresses the power and nature of hope by these words: *I shall yet praise him.* For it has the effect of elevating our thoughts to the contemplation of the grace of God, when it is hidden from our view. By the term *yet*, he confesses that for the present, and insofar as the praises of God are concerned, his mouth is stopped, seeing he is oppressed and shut up on all sides. This, however, does not prevent him from extending his hope to some future distant period; and, in order to escape from his present sorrow, and, as it were, get beyond its reach, he promises himself what as yet there was no appearance of obtaining. Nor is this an imaginary expectation produced by a fanciful mind, but, relying on the promises of God, he not only encourages himself to cherish good hope but also promises himself certain deliverance. We can only be competent witnesses to our brethren of the grace of God when, in the first place, we have borne testimony to it to our own hearts.

What follows, *the helps of his countenance*, may be differently expounded. Commentators, for the most part, supply the word *for*, so that, according to this view, David here expresses the matter or cause of thanksgiving—that *yet he would give praise or thanks to God for the help of his countenance.* This interpretation I readily admit. At the same time, the sense will not be inappropriate if we read the terms separately, thus: *helps or salvations* are *from the countenance of God.* For as soon as he is pleased to look on his people he sets them in safety. *The countenance of God* is taken for the manifestation of his favor. His countenance then appears serene and gracious to us; as, on the contrary, adversity, like the intervening clouds, darkens or obscures its benign aspect.

SECTION FIVE

————— ⚬ «(•)» ⚬ —————

Practical Dimensions

28

Why Pray?[1]

Someone will say, does God not know, even without being reminded, both in what respect we are troubled and what is expedient for us, so that it may seem in a sense superfluous that he should be stirred up by our prayers—as if he were drowsily blinking or even sleeping until he is aroused by our voice? But they who thus reason do not observe to what end the Lord instructed his people to pray, for he ordained it not so much for his own sake as for ours. Now he wills—as is right—that his due be rendered to him, in the recognition that everything men desire and account conducive to their own profit comes from him, and in the attestation of this by prayers. But the profit of this sacrifice also, by which he is worshiped, returns to us. Accordingly, the holy fathers, the more confidently they extolled God's benefits among themselves and others, were the more keenly aroused to pray. It will be enough for us to note the single example of Elijah, who, sure of God's purpose, after he has deliberately promised rain to King Ahab, still anxiously prays with his head between his knees and sends his servant seven times to look (1 Kings 18:42), not because he would discredit his prophecy, but because he knew it

---

1. Institutes 3.20.3.

was his duty, lest his faith be sleepy or sluggish, to lay his desires before God.

Therefore, even though, while we grow dull and stupid toward our miseries, he watches and keeps guard on our behalf and sometimes even helps us unasked, still it is very important for us to call on him. First, that our hearts may be fired with a zealous and burning desire ever to seek, love, and serve him, while we become accustomed in every need to flee to him as to a sacred anchor. Second, that there may enter our hearts no desire and no wish at all of which we should be ashamed to make him a witness, while we learn to set all our wishes before his eyes, and even to pour out our whole hearts. Third, that we be prepared to receive his benefits with true gratitude of heart and thanksgiving, benefits that our prayer reminds us come from his hand (cf. Ps. 145:15–16). Fourth, moreover, that, having obtained what we were seeking and being convinced that he has answered our prayers, we should be led to meditate on his kindness more ardently. And fifth, that at the same time we embrace with greater delight those things that we acknowledge to have been obtained by prayers. Finally, that use and experience may, according to the measure of our feebleness, confirm his providence, while we understand not only that he promises never to fail us and of his own will opens the way to call on him at the very point of necessity, but also that he ever extends his hand to help his own, not wet-nursing them with words but defending them with present help.

On account of these things, our most merciful Father, although he never either sleeps or idles, still very often gives the impression of one sleeping or idling in order that he may thus train us, otherwise idle and lazy, to seek, ask, and entreat him to our great good.

Therefore they act with excessive foolishness who, to call men's minds away from prayer, babble that God's providence, standing guard over all things, is vainly importuned with our entreaties, inasmuch as the Lord has not, on the contrary, vainly attested that "he is near...to all who call upon his name in truth" (Ps. 145:18). Quite like this is what others prate: that it is superfluous for them to petition for things that the Lord is gladly ready to bestow, while those very things that flow to us from his voluntary liberality he would have us recognize as granted to our prayers. That memorable saying of the psalm attests this, and to it many similar passages correspond: "For the eyes of the Lord are upon the righteous, and his ears toward their prayers" (1 Peter 3:12; Ps. 34:15). This sentence so commends the providence of God — intent of his own accord on caring for the salvation of the godly — as yet not to omit the exercise of faith, by which men's minds are cleansed of indolence. The eyes of God are therefore watchful to assist the blind in their necessity, but he is willing in turn to hear our groanings that he may the better prove his love toward us. And so both are true: "that the keeper of Israel neither slumbers nor sleeps" (Ps. 121:4), and yet that he is inactive, as if forgetting us, when he sees us idle and mute.

THOMAS CRANMER (1489–1556)

English Reformer, Archbishop of Canterbury. Calvin supported Cranmer's hope to convene a general synod to foster greater unity among Protestants, though it never came to pass. While his *Book of Common Prayer* stirred some controversy, it is unquestionably a testimony to Cranmer's commitment to piety in prayer.

29

Coming to God's Treasures[1]

"Praying with all prayer and supplication at all
times in the spirit...."
                              —Ephesians 6:18a

Many, supposing themselves to have profited well in
faith, are yet nevertheless ignorant of what belongs to
prayer. They think it enough if they can say, "God
will help us," when they see any danger at hand, and
yet they do not flee to him for refuge. But such people
do not know what purpose the promises made to us
serve. For God does not simply say to us that he will
have a care for us, and that he will undertake for us
in all our needs, but he also invites us to himself, and
at the same time encourages us in praying.

The one then cannot be separated from the other;
that is to say, if we are resting on the pledge of God's
promises and have them thoroughly rooted in our
hearts, we shall be stirred up to resort to our God, so
that our faith may exercise us in prayers and supplications. And that is why St. Paul, having told us that
the sword that is essential in the fight against Satan is
the Word of God and that the shield is faith, adds that
we ought to fight by our prayers and supplications.
Thus we see that they are inseparable things. And the
more advanced we are in faith, with the more earnest

---

1. Sermon on Ephesians 6:18–19.

zeal should we call on our God and acknowledge and confess that our salvation lies in his hand, and that we look for all good things from him.

Since we are so slothful in that respect, he sets down two words, "prayers" and "supplications," the better to express that we must not go to the work coldly, or in a way of drudgery, but that we must be touched to the quick to continue at it (as he will add soon after) and to have a true perseverance that does not grow weary. It is true that God tells us blessedly by his prophet Isaiah that he will hear us before we cry (Isa. 65:24), and his hand will be ready to succor us before we have opened our mouth. But that is not to make us slothful, that we should be waiting for him with mouth gaping, as they say, but to show that he will not permit us to be kept waiting when we have called on him, as though he were loath to help us. And for proof of it, he even goes before us, as we find by experience.

Nevertheless he will have us yield a true proof of our faith by praying to him. For the right way for us to show truly that his promises have been powerful in us and that we trust to them is that as soon as we are touched with any grief or affliction, we go straight to him and unburden our hearts there, as is said in another passage (Ps. 50:15; Ps. 62:8). Now we see how we must take advantage of God's Word, by which we are assured that he will never fail us, that is to say, by seeking in him what he assures us we shall find there. And so the prayers that we offer are, as it were, keys by which to come to the treasures that God reserves for us and that he will not keep from us. Therefore we must open the way to them by praying.

30

Praying with Confidence[1]

"And when they heard that, they lifted up their
voice to God with one accord, and said, Lord,
thou art God, which hast made heaven, and earth,
and the sea, and all that in them is.... And when
they had prayed, the place was shaken where they
were assembled together; and they were all filled
with the Holy Ghost, and they spake the word of
God with boldness."

—Acts 4:24, 31

We cannot have confidence in God as we ought
unless we are firmly convinced that he disposes of all
things in accordance with his will, so that all creatures
are subject to him. That stems from the fact that he
created all things. We have to know that, owing to his
authority and preeminence, everything in heaven and
on earth is in his hand and is upheld by his power and
might. Therefore we need to take note of two things.
The first is that if we are to pray to God certain that he
will answer us, we must not doubt his power, and we
must know nothing can keep him from helping us and
delivering us from all the dangers that might befall
us. So if we have that kind of confidence when we
approach God, we will never fail to pray effectively.

---

1. Sermon on Acts 4:24, 31.

The second is that we must be assured of the power of God, which we can ponder not only in the creation of the world, but also in its continuation. Our Lord did not just create the heaven and the earth and all they contain only to relinquish his rights as though he were no longer interested in taking care of it. Creation must always be sustained by his power; otherwise, it could not continue for a single minute. Therefore, since our Lord holds all created things in his hand, let us not doubt that he is sufficient to preserve us and lead us in all our undertakings, provided we turn to him alone.

It is not enough to have experienced the power of God. We must add to it his promises, by which he conveys his benevolent will and love toward us. Those who address the power of God and only create a fantasy in their minds without considering his promises and the goodness that he has exercised from all time and still wishes to exercise toward us—they and all their imaginings will reap only condemnation. It is true that when we think about God's exalted majesty, we are not thunderstruck. But to be truly certain, we must come to the knowledge that God is all-powerful and wishes to fulfill all his promises to us. When we are in possession of these two things, we have the right introduction to praying effectively.

31

Prayer, Forgiveness,
and Repentance[1]

The beginning, and even the preparation, of proper
prayer is the plea for pardon with a humble and
sincere confession of guilt. No one, however holy
he may be, should hope that he will obtain anything
from God until he is freely reconciled to him; nor can
God chance to be propitious to any but those whom
he has pardoned.

Accordingly, it is no wonder if believers open
for themselves the door to prayer with this key, as
we learn from numerous passages of the Psalms.
For David, asking for something else than remission of his sins, says: "Remember not the sins of
my youth, and my transgressions; according to
thy mercy remember me, for thy goodness' sake,
O LORD" (Ps. 25:7). Again: "See my affliction
and my toil, and forgive all my sins" (Ps. 25:18).
Also, in this we see that it is not enough for us to
call ourselves to account each day for recent sins
if we do not remember those sins that might seem
to have been long forgotten.

For the same prophet, elsewhere having confessed
one grave offense, on that occasion even turns back

---

1. Institutes 3.20.9.

to his mother's womb, in which he had contracted the infection (Ps. 51:5), not to extenuate the guilt on the ground of corruption of nature but that, in gathering up the sins of his whole life, the more rigorously he condemns himself, the more easily entreated he may find God. But even though the saints do not always beg forgiveness of sins in so many words, if we diligently ponder their prayers that Scripture relates, we shall readily come upon what I speak of: that they have received their intention to pray from God's mercy alone, and thus always have begun with appeasing him. For if anyone should question his own conscience, he would be so far from daring intimately to lay aside his tares before God that, unless he relied on mercy and pardon, he would tremble at every approach.

There is also another special confession when suppliants ask release from punishments. It is that at the same time they may pray for the pardon of their sins. For it would be absurd to wish the effect to be removed while the cause remained. We must guard against imitating foolish sick folk, who, concerned solely with the treatment of symptoms, neglect the very root of the disease. We must make it our first concern that God be favorable toward us, rather than that he attest his favor by outward signs, because he wills to maintain this order, and it would have been of small profit to us to have him do us good unless our conscience, feeling him wholly appeased, rendered him altogether lovely (Song of Sol. 5:16). Christ's reply also reminds us of this, for after he had decided to heal the paralytic, "Your sins," he said, "are forgiven you" (Matt. 9:2). He thus arouses our minds to what we ought especially to desire: that God may receive us into grace; then, that in aiding us he may set forth the fruit of reconciliation.

But besides that special confession of present guilt with which believers plead for the remission of every sin and penalty, the general preface that gains favor for prayers must never be passed over, for unless they are founded in free mercy, prayers never reach God. John's statement can be applied to this: "If we confess our sins, he is faithful and just to forgive us our sins, and to cleanse us from all unrighteousness" (1 John 1:9). For this reason, under the law prayers had to be consecrated with blood atonement (Gen. 12:8; 26:25; 33:20; 1 Sam. 7:9) in order that they should be accepted, and that the people should thus be warned that they were unworthy of so great a privilege of honor until, purged of their defilement, they derived confidence in prayer solely from God's mercy.

JOHANNES OECOLAMPADIUS (1482–1531)

German Reformer, ministered in Basel. Was an
associate of Erasmus, and came to the Reformed
faith. He became an associate of Zwingli in the Swiss
Reformation. He provided an early critique of the
Roman Catholic practice of public confession and
penance.

32

Turning to God from the Heart[1]

"Repent, and be baptized everyone of you in the name of Jesus Christ for the remission of sins, and you shall receive the gift of the Holy Spirit."

—Acts 2:38

After the Jews acknowledged their fault and declared openly they would do whatever the apostles told them, Peter adds God's counsel: "Repent." In Psalm 51 we read that a contrite heart and a broken spirit are a sacrifice pleasing to God, and that he never rejects the one who comes to him in such humility (v. 19). God greatly consoles us by assuring us that if we come to him in sorrow for offending him, he will accept that contrition as a sweet-smelling sacrifice; he will receive us and sanctify us by his grace. And that very consolation should stir us to repentance. But there are very few who think about that, because sins reign too much in us, and the devil intoxicates us or, rather, charms us so much that we do not think about the perdition that is on our doorstep. Nevertheless, the fact remains that we do well to be affected by our Lord's readiness to receive us if we go to him in repentance.

---

1. Sermon on Acts 2:38.

Let us consider now that when God disposes us to come to him, we must do so immediately, just as Peter tells the Jews: "Repent, and be baptized everyone of you in the name of Jesus Christ for the remission of sins, and you shall receive the gift of the Holy Spirit" (Acts 2:38). So we have here Peter's first point, which is like an exhortation to the Jews to repent; the second is a promise of the remission of sins. The third is to show the remission of our sins must be founded on the name of Jesus Christ, and the fourth is the witness of the remission of our sins—namely, baptism. That is what we must declare.

To understand each point more easily, we need to know what repentance is.... It is, in a word, the turning of a man to God. For by nature we are alienated from God and can do nothing but the things he condemns. That, therefore, is the condition of man in himself—that is, a condition totally repugnant to the righteousness of God. Now here is God calling us to himself by repentance. Take the case of a man whose back was turned on God. When God in his grace gives him knowledge of his sin through the preaching of his Word and so brings him to repentance, he then turns around and contemplates God face to face. In that, we see repentance does not lie in outward nonsensical actions, such as abstaining from eating meats on one day rather than on another.... But repentance has its seat in the spirit and in the heart. That is why we must pay close attention to what we have touched on. For when we come to God, will we come with feet or hands or tongue? Not at all! The heart must work at it. And in fact, this word, as used in Scripture, tells us mainly that we have become new creatures (2 Cor. 5:17).

So we see now both how repentance encompasses man's turning to God and how its principal seat lies in the heart and in the spirit. And that is why Scripture, when speaking of our conversion, also confronts us with the weakness of our flesh: the old man must be put to death (Eph. 4:22–24); that is, the nature with which we are born as human beings must be removed, for there is only wickedness in us. Therefore, we must begin by blaming ourselves and by conquering what constitutes our own condition. Then, God must rule in us and cover us with his grace, for it would not be enough for us to be put to death if God did not give us a new life so that he might use us entirely in his service. And this is how we can experience repentance: it is when God gives us the grace to bring all our desires into captivity, when all that makes up our human nature is conquered and we are so governed by his Holy Spirit that our lives are completely ruled by his word, whereas formerly we were devoted to evil.

HULDREICH ZWINGLI (1484–1531)

Swiss Reformer, ministered in Zurich. Was the leading figure of reform in Switzerland, yet was unable to bring unity between the Lutherans and Reformed churches.

33

Seizing Repentance[1]

"Repent, and be baptized everyone of you in the name of Jesus Christ for the remission of sins, and you shall receive the gift of the Holy Spirit."

—Acts 2:38

Our nature is so fertile for evil that it always produces a new vice, and our Lord has no sooner removed one vice from us than the process must be repeated. For vices well up within us one after another like water from a fountain. So then we need to try hard every day to repent so as to return more effectively to the will of God. And that is a thing badly practiced (although it is very necessary), for we do not think about our sins to abandon them or remember the will of God to follow it. And yet each one of us, man or woman, must try daily to consider: "Well now, how have I conducted my life up till now? How have I used the fear of God to advantage? I find that each day requires a new beginning, for I do not chastise myself for some admonition or other I may receive." That is how we must examine ourselves. When we experience this sorrow for offending God, we must not doubt that our Lord supplies what lacks and

---

1. Sermon on Acts 2:38.

thereby brings us to the true repentance mentioned here. That is the way we must approach him. Otherwise, if we ever think we take one step closer to him, we take two steps back.

Now we must not be surprised if we are unable to prick our own conscience, because we do the very opposite. We are grieved if someone speaks of our vices in public. We do not want anyone to reproach us for them. We do not want to think about them in private either. And yet Solomon says—and not without cause—that the man who is often afraid is blessed (Prov. 28:14), not that we should be afraid of putting ourselves in such defiance that we cannot return to God, but that we should be quick to confront our vice head on and take heed to correct it while God gives us the grace to put our mind to it. Now since very few of us do that and are blessed, many more of us do not do that and are not blessed. And no matter how much we boast of being Christian, we indicate clearly, unless we change our ways, that ours is but empty boasting.

For we should know that Christian teaching consists of these two points: namely, repentance and the remission of sins. We have no other instruction from God. After Jesus Christ instructed his apostles, he said, "Preach repentance and the remission of sins" (Luke 24:47). We must be refashioned through repentance if we wish to receive remission of our sins. For up to that point, we shall not be able to lean on God's goodness and entrust ourselves to him as we should. And that is why we see many people who are far from being Christians. For, as I said earlier concerning repentance, they never want to acquire knowledge of their sins and do not want to be badgered about them, and yet it is in repentance that all our well-being lies. May we, through the reproofs directed against us, be able to seize this repentance that will let us taste the goodness of God so that we may entrust ourselves entirely to him.

GASPAR DE COLIGNY (1519–1572)

French admiral, became a devoted Huguenot. He attempted to create French colonies and missions outposts in Brazil and Florida, and was martyred during the St. Bartholomew's Day massacre. His correspondence with Calvin reveals how his sufferings drew him close to God, having him see service to God's will as more comforting than his own.

34

Belonging to God rather than Ourselves[1]

Even though the law of the Lord provides the finest and best disposed method of ordering a man's life, it seemed good to the Heavenly Teacher to shape his people by an even more explicit plan to that rule that he had set forth in the law. Here, then, is the beginning of this plan: the duty of believers is "to present their bodies to God as a living sacrifice, holy and acceptable to him," and in this consists the lawful worship of him (Rom. 12:1). From this is derived the basis of the exhortation that "they be not conformed to the fashion of this world, but be transformed by the renewal of their minds, so that they may prove what is the will of God" (Rom. 12:2). Now the great thing is this: we are consecrated and dedicated to God in order that we may thereafter think, speak, meditate, and do nothing except to his glory. For a sacred thing may not be applied to profane uses without marked injury to him. If we, then, are not our own (cf. 1 Cor. 6:19) but the Lord's, it is clear what error we must flee, and whither we must direct all the acts of our life.

We are not our own: let not our reason nor our will, therefore, sway our plans and deeds. We are not

---

1. Institutes 3.7.1.

our own: let us therefore not set it as our goal to seek what is expedient for us according to the flesh. We are not our own: insofar as we can, let us therefore forget ourselves and all that is ours. Conversely, we are God's: let us therefore live for him and die for him. We are God's: let his wisdom and will therefore rule all our actions. We are God's: let all the parts of our life accordingly strive toward him as our only lawful goal (Rom. 14:8; cf. 1 Cor. 6:19). Oh, how much has that man profited who, having been taught that he is not his own, has taken away dominion and rule from his own reason that he may yield it to God! For, since consulting our self-interest is the pestilence that most effectively leads to our destruction, so the sole haven of salvation is to be wise in nothing and to will nothing through ourselves but to follow the leading of the Lord alone.

Let this therefore be the first step: that a man depart from himself in order that he may apply the whole force of his ability in the service of the Lord. I call "service" not only what lies in obedience to God's Word but what turns the mind of man, empty of its own carnal sense, wholly to the bidding of God's Spirit. While it is the first entrance to life, all philosophers were ignorant of this transformation, which Paul calls "renewal of the mind" (Eph. 4:23). For they set up reason alone as the ruling principle in man and think that it alone should be listened to; to it alone, in short, they entrust the conduct of life. But the Christian philosophy bids reason give way to, submit and subject itself to, the Holy Spirit so that the man himself may no longer live but hear Christ living and reigning within him (Gal. 2:20).

35

———— ✦ ————

Controlling Our Carnal Affections[1]

"And they stoned Stephen calling upon God,
and saying, Lord Jesus, receive my spirit. And he
kneeled down, and cried with a loud voice, Lord,
lay not this sin to their charge. And when he had
said this, he fell asleep."

—Acts 7:59–60

It should be our responsibility to exercise control
over all our carnal affections, just like holding back
wild animals on leashes and keeping them captive.
We will never be able to yield ourselves to God's
service until we have forcibly restrained our human
nature, because all the affections of our flesh and all
our thoughts, as Paul says, are just so many enemies
working against God (Rom. 8:7; Eph. 2:3). All the
desires, all the wicked thoughts that can assail man,
are like soldiers at war with God and his truth. As
a result, we will never be disposed to dedicate ourselves completely to God and his service until we
learn to put our human nature to death, so wretched
and accursed is it.

But, as I have said, very few will go to such
trouble. To the contrary. Everyone delights in his
own vices. We think it is enough to say, "We are not

---

1. Sermon on Acts 7:58–60.

angels and we are not that perfect." Well, if we are not angels, God will destroy us along with the devils if we are unwilling to come into line with his will. It is true that no man is so perfect that he can love his enemies the way Jesus Christ does. But the fact is we must strive to do so by putting to death all our wicked affections, because we know they are God's enemies. To that end we have to pray not only for all people in general but also for our enemies. And yet few are they who do it.

But what is worse, there are many who, when done some wrong, are not content to seek vengeance and return evil for evil. If anyone tries to rebuke them for their sins, they think they have been gravely injured. That is a great pity. I do not know how most people can avoid feeling shame when they call themselves Christian, since that impudence is the rule everywhere. It is a common practice when our vices are reproved that those who realize their guilt most keenly think they have been deeply offended and want to inflict an ignominious punishment upon the offender. In fact, some discontented people are so incensed they complain because they are unable to spew their venom. Against whom? Against those whom they have accused of rebuking them.

In short, if someone tries to rebuke sins in our day and time, he needs to make an appointment with death at the same time — as if he had committed some grievous offence. But, as I have said, if someone has rebuked a person in order to show him his faults, the rebuked person needs to make peace and say, "I forgive him for offending me." And what did that person who was appointed by God do to you?

He rebuked you for your sin, as he was obliged to do, and he must be forgiven. But because he has tried to rebuke sins, everybody comes and takes sides against him. And what does that say about our progress? It is still a common problem among us today.

WOLFGANG MUSCULUS (1497–1563)

German Reformer, studied in Strasbourg, ministered in Augsburg, forced out of Germany by the Augsburg Interim (1548), and became a professor of theology at Berne. Calvin hoped that his friend's appointment in Berne would ease tensions between Berne and Geneva.

36

Fighting Against Our Natural Inclinations[1]

"Fight the good fight of faith."
—1 Timothy 6:12a

Even though a Christian keeps himself under control, he must fight in order to stand steadfast in the faith. That is because there is nothing more contrary to our nature than to forgo these earthly things and not to be preoccupied by them, but to seek instead with all our hearts and souls the things that are unseen, that are completely hidden from our eyes and far beyond the reach of our senses. The faithful Christian must look higher than himself when there is any question of thinking about the kingdom of God and eternal life. And yet we know how our minds are inclined towards the things we have in our hands. How, then, is it possible for us to stand firm in the faith unless we resist and strive boldly against all our natural inclinations? And so, when we meet with these temptations and are stirred up to fight, let us take this doctrine of St. Paul as our shield—namely, that faith is never without a fight, that we can never serve God without being soldiers. Why? Because we have enemies before

---

1. Sermon on 1 Timothy 6:12–14.

us and we are surrounded on every side. And therefore we must get used to fighting, or else we shall be forced to surrender. Since this is so, that no one can serve God without exercising patience in the midst of the afflictions by which the children of God are afflicted, let us beware lest we renounce our faith, but let us still press on.

I could wish that I were able to employ myself wholly in praising God joyfully and to be contented and at peace; that I were not troubled by men, but that all my senses were inclined to do well. This would be what I would wish for; yet God will try me, and my fiercest battles must be against my own natural inclinations. And when the devil mounts many combats against me, when temptations come on all sides, I must beware lest I should be overcome; I must stand firm, and I must be strong and steadfast. And so I must not be weak in this situation, or I shall be in danger of renouncing my faith. And what a thing that would be—to forsake my faith, to which God has called me! So let us go on, and not think it strange that this life is full of so many assaults, and that we must withstand many enemies, and that we need from day to day to get more strength to submit to this situation in which God would place us.

37

Christ's Cross and Ours[1]

It behooves the godly mind to climb still higher [than self-denial], to the height to which Christ calls his disciples: that each must bear his own cross (Matt. 16:24). For whoever the Lord has adopted and deemed worthy of his fellowship ought to prepare themselves for a hard, toilsome, and unquiet life, crammed with very many and various kinds of evil. It is the heavenly Father's will thus to exercise them so as to put his own children to a definite test. Beginning with Christ, his firstborn, he follows this plan with all his children. For even though that Son was beloved above the rest, and in him the Father's mind was well pleased (Matt. 3:17 and 17:5), yet we see that far from being treated indulgently or softly (to speak the truth), while he dwelt on earth he was not only tried by a perpetual cross but his whole life was nothing but a sort of perpetual cross. The apostle notes the reason: that it behooved him to "learn obedience through what he suffered" (Heb. 5:8).

Why should we exempt ourselves, therefore, from the condition to which Christ our Head had to submit, especially since he submitted to it for our sake, to show us an example of patience in himself? Therefore, the apostle teaches that God has destined

---

1. Institutes 3.8.1–2.

all his children to the end that they be conformed to Christ (Rom. 8:29). Hence also in harsh and difficult conditions, regarded as adverse and evil, a great comfort comes to us: we share Christ's sufferings in order that, as he has passed from a labyrinth of all evils into heavenly glory, we may in like manner be led through various tribulations to the same glory (Acts 14:22). So Paul himself elsewhere states: when we come to know the sharing of his sufferings, we at the same time grasp the power of his resurrection; and when we become like him in his death, we are thus made ready to share his glorious resurrection (Phil. 3:10–11). How much can it do to soften all the bitterness of the cross, that the more we are afflicted with adversities, the more surely our fellowship with Christ is confirmed! By communion with him the very sufferings themselves not only become blessed to us but also help much in promoting our salvation.

Besides this, our Lord had no need to undertake the bearing of the cross except to attest and prove his obedience to the Father. But as for us, there are many reasons why we must pass our lives under a continual cross. First, since we are by nature too inclined to attribute everything to our flesh—unless our feebleness be shown, as it were, to our eyes—we readily esteem our virtue above its due measure. And we do not doubt, whatever happens, that against all difficulties it will remain unbroken and unconquered. Hence we are lifted up into stupid and empty confidence in the flesh, and relying on it, we are then insolently proud against God himself, as if our own powers were sufficient without his grace.

He can best restrain this arrogance when he proves to us by experience not only the great incapacity but also the frailty under which we labor. Therefore, he afflicts us either with disgrace or poverty, or bereavement, or disease, or other calamities. Utterly unequal to bearing these, insofar as they touch us, we soon succumb to them. Thus humbled, we learn to call on his power, which alone makes us stand fast under the weight of afflictions. But even the most holy persons, however much they may recognize that they stand not through their own strength but through God's grace, are too sure of their own fortitude and constancy unless by the testing of the cross he brings them into a deeper knowledge of himself. This complacency even stole upon David: "In my tranquility I said, 'I shall never be moved.' O Jehovah, by thy favor thou hadst established strength for my mountain; thou didst hide thy face, I was dismayed" (Ps. 30:6–7). For he confesses that in prosperity his senses had been so benumbed with sluggishness that, neglecting God's grace, on which he ought to have depended, he so relied on himself as to promise himself he could ever stand fast. If this happened to so great a prophet, what one of us should not be afraid and take care?

PRINCESS RENÉE (1510–1574)

Duchess of Ferrara, daughter of Louis XII, King of France, and sister-in-law of Francis I, King of France. Early in his career, Calvin hoped to serve as her secretary, but had to return to France. The two maintained a correspondence for years to come. Calvin admired her for standing firm in faith during constant persecution.

38

Taking Refuge in God[1]

"But he [Stephen], being full of the Holy Ghost, looked up stedfastly into heaven, and saw the glory of God, and Jesus standing on the right hand of God."

—Acts 7:55

Now it is worth noting that Luke says, "Stephen, being filled with the Holy Spirit, saw the glory of God and of Jesus Christ," which he says to point out our need to be led by the Spirit of God. Even though his glory is quite apparent, we will not see it any better than blind men unless the Holy Spirit fills us and opens our eyes. That is what Stephen wanted to point out. But in order to glean the substance of the teaching contained in this passage, we must first notice that Stephen points out that we must take refuge in God when we are in extreme affliction and see only men's fury and rage against us. That is the only remedy that can give us assurance—namely, that we totally entrust ourselves and our undertaking to God.

Our Lord has a reason for declaring that he will help his people in time of need. It is true that we always need his help and that he is also ready to provide it. And he particularly declares that he will

---

1. Sermon on Acts 7:52–56.

sustain us whenever we are oppressed by evil and afflicted on all sides, and that it is at those times that he will show he is even nearer. So let us learn from Stephen's example that when we are in confusion in this life and surrounded on all sides and so heavily oppressed that we can take no more, God will manifest his help at that time, declaring to us that that is the way he wants to draw us to himself, provided he is our sole refuge. That then is a primary teaching of this passage that we must take to heart. The teaching deserves greater elaboration, but let us look to applying it to our instruction, and although we are dealing with it in few words, let us not fail to imbibe it and profit from it.

In the first place, when some evil presses on us, when men persecute us, and when we are tormented in some way or another, let us follow Stephen's example and turn to God as he did in this passage, and we will find that God will help us even better than we hoped. However, as I have said, we must be filled with the Holy Spirit. Not that we might have him as fully as Stephen did, but the fact is that if the Holy Spirit does not appear to us and give us the ability to see, we will never glimpse God's glory—provided we do not think God grants us the grace to contemplate him without first enlightening us by his Holy Spirit. There is a difference between God and us; we cannot reach him; we cannot have the minutest knowledge of him unless he cleanses us of all our wicked affections. And how will he do that? By his Holy Spirit.

39

Lining Up for Combat[1]

"As many as desire to make a fair shew in the flesh,
they constrain you to be circumcised; only lest they
should suffer persecution for the cross of Christ."
—Galatians 6:12

If we desire to serve God and his church, we must
always be prepared to undergo danger. Even though
the fires are not lit, and the enemies are not armed to
execute the cruel persecution that they would like to
mete out (or rather, even though our Lord is restrain-
ing those who are furious with his Word, and who
wish to throw off his yoke), yet we must, nevertheless, suffer the revilings of many people. We will
be defamed; there will be murmurings and slanders
against us; but let us breathe it all in and then harden
ourselves against it, as it were. We see that wherever
the gospel is preached, a thousand accusations come
against those who seek to carry out their duty faithfully. They are put on trial and accused of this and
that, but it is all pure calumny. In short, all those who
wish to pursue their course must prepare themselves
to bear many trials; these would lead them to compro-
mise, were they not determined to obey God despite
everyone else. Here is one thing.

---

1. Sermon on Galatians 6:12–13.

However, we ought to remember that this extends to the whole body of the church in general. When we hear the message of peace that is brought to us in the name of God, let us not expect to be at rest as regards this world, but always to have to deal with many quarrels and difficulties. If anyone is not prepared for this, he must leave the Lord Jesus Christ, for such a person can never be one of his disciples. As he declares with his own mouth, the one who does not bend his shoulders to carry his burden and his cross is not worthy to be in his school, and indeed all such are excluded (Matt. 10:38). Therefore, let us learn that, being called to the Lord Jesus Christ, we must share in his cross as much as pleases him; as it is written, that if we suffer with him, we will also be glorified and partake of the power that was revealed at his resurrection (Rom. 6:5). We must still have fulfilled in us, as members of his body, the sufferings that he first endured. It is true that he alone suffered what was necessary for our salvation, but we need to be conformed to his image, as it says in the eighth chapter to the Romans.

However, even if God spares us from being amongst tyrants who could torture us, or evil men who could attack us, and he ensures that they only bark at us—yes, even if he leaves us in peace—it is because he pities our frailty and spares us because of our weakness. Let us not flatter ourselves in this meanwhile, but let us pray to God that through his Holy Spirit he would strengthen us. Then, when he calls us to line up ready for combat, we will not act like raw recruits but will have premeditated long since the fact that we must share in the sufferings of Jesus Christ in order to reach the glory of his resurrection.

40

Resting in God's Will[1]

Trust in God's blessing only

Suppose we believe that every means toward a prosperous and desirable outcome rests on the blessing of God alone; and that, when this is absent, all sorts of misery and calamity dog us. It remains for us not greedily to strive after riches and honors—whether relying on our own dexterity of wit or our own diligence, or depending on the favor of men, or having confidence in vainly imagined fortune—but for us always to look to the Lord so that by his guidance we may be led to whatever lot he has provided for us. Thus it will first come to pass that we shall not dash out to seize on riches and usurp honors through wickedness and by stratagems and evil arts, or greed, to the injury of our neighbors, but [we shall] pursue only those enterprises that do not lead us away from innocence.

Who can hope for the help of a divine blessing amidst frauds, robberies, and other wicked arts? For since that blessing follows only him who thinks purely and acts rightly, thus it calls back from crooked thoughts and wicked actions all those who seek it. Then will a bridle be put on us that we may not burn with an immoderate desire to grow rich or ambitiously

1. Institute 3.7.9–10.

pant after honors. For with what shamelessness does a man trust that he will be helped by God to obtain those things that he desires contrary to God's Word? Away with the thought that God would abet with his blessing what he curses with his mouth!

Lastly, if things do not go according to our wish and hope, we will still be restrained from impatience and loathing of our condition, whatever it may be. For we shall know that this is to murmur against God, by whose will riches and poverty, contempt and honor, are dispensed. To sum up, he who rests solely on the blessing of God as it has been here expressed will neither strive with evil arts after those things that men customarily madly seek after, which he realizes will not profit him, nor will he, if things go well, give credit to himself or even to his diligence, or industry, or fortune. Rather, he will give God the credit as its Author. But if, while other men's affairs flourish, he makes but slight advancement, or even slips back, he will still bear his low estate with greater equanimity and moderation of mind than some profane person would bear a moderate success that merely does not correspond with his wish. For he indeed possesses a solace in which he may repose more peacefully than in the highest degree of wealth or power. Since this leads to his salvation, he considers that his affairs are ordained by the Lord. We see that David was so minded; while he follows God and gives himself over to his leading, he attests that he is like a child weaned from his mother's breast, and that he does not occupy himself with things too deep and wonderful for him (Ps. 131:1–2).

Self-denial helps us bear adversity

And for godly minds the peace and forbearance we have spoken of ought not to rest solely in this point, but it must also be extended to every occurrence to which the present life is subject. Therefore, he alone has duly denied himself who has so totally resigned himself to the Lord that he permits every part of his life to be governed by God's will. He who will be thus composed in mind, whatever happens, will not consider himself miserable nor complain of his lot with ill will toward God. How necessary this disposition is will appear if you weigh the many chance happenings to which we are subject. Various diseases repeatedly trouble us: now plague rages; now we are cruelly beset by the calamities of war; now ice and hail, consuming the year's expectation, lead to barrenness, which reduces us to poverty; wife, parents, children, neighbors are snatched away by death; our house is burned by fire. It is on account of these occurrences that men curse their life, loathe the day of their birth, abominate heaven and the light of day, rail against God, and, since they are eloquent in blasphemy, accuse him of injustice and cruelty.

But in these matters the believer must also look to God's kindness and truly fatherly indulgence. Accordingly, if he sees his house reduced to solitude by the removal of his kinsfolk, he will not indeed even then cease to bless the Lord but rather will turn his attention to this thought: nevertheless, the grace of the Lord, which dwells in my house, will not leave it desolate. Or, if his crops are blasted by frost, or destroyed by ice, or beaten down with hail, and he sees famine threatening, yet he will not despair or bear a grudge against God, but will remain firm in this trust (cf. Ps. 78:47): "Nevertheless we are in the Lord's protection, sheep brought up in his pastures" (Ps. 79:13). The Lord will therefore supply food to us even in extreme barrenness. If he shall be afflicted by disease, he will not even then be so unmanned by the harshness of pain as to break forth into impatience and expostulate with God; but, by considering the righteousness and gentleness of God's chastening, he will recall himself to forbearance. In short, whatever happens, because he will know it is ordained of God, he will undergo it with a peaceful and grateful mind, so as not obstinately to resist the command of him into whose power he once for all surrendered himself and his every possession.

41

Cherishing Moderation[1]

It is expedient here to discuss briefly to what end
Scripture teaches that all things are divinely ordained.
Three things, indeed, are to be noted. First, God's
providence must be considered with regard to the
future as well as the past. Second, it is the deter-
minative principle of all things in such a way that
sometimes it works through an intermediary, sometimes without an intermediary, sometimes contrary to
every intermediary. Finally, it strives to the end that
God may reveal his concern for the whole human
race, but especially his vigilance in ruling the church,
which he deigns to watch more closely. Now this,
also, ought to be added: that although either fatherly
favor and beneficence or severity of judgment often
shine forth in the whole course of providence, nevertheless sometimes the causes of the events are hidden.
So the thought creeps in that human affairs turn and
whirl at the blind urge of fortune, or the flesh incites
us to contradiction, as if God were making sport of
men by throwing them about like balls.

It is, indeed, true that if we had quiet and composed minds ready to learn, the final outcome would
show that God always has the best reason for his
plan: either to instruct his own people in patience, or

---

1. Institutes 1.17.1.

to correct their wicked affections and tame their lust, or to subjugate them to self-denial, or to arouse them from sluggishness; again, to bring low the proud, to shatter the cunning of the impious and to overthrow their devices. Yet however hidden and fugitive from our point of view the causes may be, we must hold that they are surely laid up with him, and hence we must exclaim with David, "Great, O God, are the wondrous deeds that thou hast done, and thy thoughts toward us cannot be reckoned; if I try to speak, they would be more than can be told" (Ps. 40:5). For even though in our miseries our sins ought always to come to mind, [so] that punishment itself may incite us to repentance, yet we see how Christ claims for the Father's secret plan a broader justice than simply punishing each one as he deserves. For concerning the man born blind he says, "Neither he nor his parents sinned, but that God's glory may be manifested in him" (John 9:3). For here our nature cries out, when calamity comes before birth itself, as if God with so little mercy thus punished the undeserving. Yet Christ testifies that in this miracle the glory of his Father shines, provided our eyes be pure.

But we must so cherish moderation that we do not try to make God render account to us, but so reverence his secret judgments as to consider his will the truly just cause of all things. When dense clouds darken the sky and a violent tempest arises, because a gloomy mist is cast over our eyes, thunder strikes our ears and all our senses are benumbed with fright, everything seems to us to be confused and mixed up; but all the while a constant quiet and serenity ever remain in heaven. So must we infer that, while the disturbances in the world deprive us of judgment, God out of the pure light of his justice and wisdom tempers and directs these very movements in the best-conceived order to a right end. And surely on this point it is sheer folly that many dare with greater license to call God's works to account, and to examine his secret plans, and to pass as rash a sentence on matters unknown as they would on the deeds of mortal men. For what is more absurd than to use this moderation toward our equals, that we prefer to suspend judgment rather than be charged with rashness, yet [we] haughtily revile the hidden judgments of God, which we ought to hold in reverence?

IDELETTE DE BURE (ca. 1499–1549)

Wife of Calvin. When she died, Calvin wrote to Viret, "I have been bereaved of the best companion of my life, of one who, had it been so ordered, would not only have been the willing sharer of my indigence, but even of my death. During her life she was the faithful helper of my ministry. From her I never experienced the slightest hindrance."

42

Remaining at Leisure for
God's Service[1]

"He that is married careth for the things of
the world."
— 1 Corinthians 7:33a

By *the things of the world* you must understand the
things that belong to the present life, for "the world"
is taken here to mean the condition of this earthly
life. But from this someone will infer that all, therefore, who are married are strangers to the kingdom
of God, as thinking of nothing but this earth. I
answer that the apostle speaks only of a portion of
the thoughts, as though he had said, "They have one
eye directed to the Lord, but in such a way as to have
the other directed to their wife. For marriage is like a
burden by which the mind of a pious man is weighed
down, so that he does not move Godward with so
much alacrity."

Let us always, however, bear in mind, that these
evils do not belong to marriage but proceed from the
depravity of men. Hence the calumnies of Jerome,
who scrapes together all these things for the purpose
of bringing marriages into disrepute, fall. For were
anyone to condemn agriculture, merchandise, and
other modes of life on this ground — that amidst so

---

1. *Commentary* on 1 Corinthians 7:33.

many corruptions of the world, there is not one of them that is exempt from certain evils — who is there that would not smile at his folly? Observe, then, that whatever evil there is in marriage has its origin somewhere else. For at this day a man would not have been turned away from the Lord by the society of his wife, if he had remained in a state of innocence and had not corrupted the holy institution of God; but a wife would have been a *helpmeet* to him in everything good, since she was created for that end (Gen. 2:18).

But some one will say, "If anxieties that are faulty and blameworthy are invariably connected with marriage, how is it possible for married persons to call on God and serve him with a pure conscience?" I answer that there are *three* kinds of anxieties. There are some that are evil and wicked in themselves, because they spring from distrust. Of these Christ speaks in Matthew 6:25. There are others that are necessary and are not displeasing to God: as, for example, it becomes the father of a family to be concerned for his wife and children, and God does not mean that we should be mere stumps, so as to have no concern as to ourselves. The *third* class are a mixture of the two former, when we are anxious respecting those things as to which we ought to feel anxiety, but [we] feel too keenly excited, in consequence of that excess that is natural to us. Such anxieties, therefore, are not by any means wrong in themselves, but they are corrupt in consequence of…undo excess. And the apostle did not intend merely to condemn here those vices by which we contract guilt in the sight of God, but he desires in a general way that we may be freed from all pediments, so as to be wholly at leisure for the service of God.

43

Obeying God's Will[1]

"All things surely are clean to them that are clean, but unto them that are defiled, and unto the unbelieving nothing is clean, but even their minds and consciences are defiled. They confess they know God, but they deny him by their works: seeing they are abominable and unbelievers, and reprobate to every good work."

—Titus 1:15–16

If we wish to know how our life should be regulated, let us examine the contents of the Word of God. For we cannot be sanctified by outward show and pomp, although they are so highly esteemed among men. We must call on God in sincerity and put our whole trust in him; we must give up pride and presumption and resort to him with true lowliness of mind, that we be not given to fleshly affections. We must endeavor to hold ourselves in awe, under subjection to God, and flee from gluttony, whoredom, excess, robbery, blasphemy, and other evils. Thus we see what God would have us do, in order to have our life well regulated.

When men would justify themselves by outward works, it is like covering a heap of filth with a clean

---

1. Sermon on Titus 1:15–16.

linen cloth. Therefore, let us put away the filthiness that is hidden in our hearts; I say, let us drive the evil from us, and then the Lord will accept of our life: thus we may see wherein consists the true knowledge of God! When we understand this aright, it will lead us to live in obedience to his will. Men have not become so beastly as to have no understanding that there is a God who created them. But this knowledge, if they do not submit to his requirements, serves as a condemnation to them, because their eyes are blindfolded by Satan, insomuch that although the gospel may be preached to them, they do not understand it. In this situation we see many at the present day. How many there are in the world who have been taught by the doctrine of the gospel and yet continue in brutish ignorance!

This happens because Satan hath so prepossessed the minds of men with wicked affections that although the light may shine ever so bright, they still remain blind and see nothing at all. Let us learn, then, that the true knowledge of God is of such a nature that it shows itself and yields fruit through our whole life. Therefore to know God, as St. Paul said to the Corinthians, we must be transformed into his image. For if we pretend to know him, and in the meantime our life be loose and wicked, it needs no witness to prove us liars; our own life bears sufficient record that we are mockers and falsifiers, and that we abuse the name of God.

St. Paul says in another place, "If ye know Jesus Christ, ye must put off the old man"—as if he should say, "We cannot declare that we know Jesus Christ, only by acknowledging him for our head, and by his receiving us as his members," which cannot be done until we have cast off the old man and become new creatures. The world hath at all times abused God's name wickedly, as it doth still at this day; therefore, let us have an eye to the true knowledge of the Word of God, whereof St. Paul speaks.

Finally, let us not put our own works into the balance and say they are good, and that we think well of them; but let us understand that the good works are those that God hath commanded in his law and that all we can do beside these are nothing. Therefore, let us learn to shape our lives according to what God hath commanded: to put our trust in him, to call on him, to give him thanks, to bear patiently whatsoever it pleases him to send us, to deal uprightly with our neighbors, and to live honestly before all men. These are the works that God requires at our hands.

JAN ŁASKI (1499–1560)

Polish Reformer, ministered in Emden, London, and became secretary to Sigismund II, King of Poland. He corresponded with Calvin and sought to maintain an international coalition of Reformed churches.

44

Honoring God and Living Justly[1]

"These are the words which the LORD spake to your multitude, upon the mount from the midst of the fire, out of the cloud and darkness, with a great voice. And he added no more thereunto, but wrote them in two tables of stone, and gave them unto me."

—Deuteronomy 5:22

Does man really want to rule his life in complete perfection? If so, in the first place, it is necessary for him to yield to the service of God in order to know what God requires and approves, and then we should live in such justice and equity with our neighbors that we demonstrate thereby that we are true children of God. Therefore the first requires that we acknowledge that God wants be honored by us; the second, that we render to our neighbors what belongs to them and observe the natural law of not doing anything to anyone unless we would want them to do the same to us.

Accordingly, in one table God has explained how he willed to be served, as we have shown earlier, putting himself in a category by himself, in order that we might not make new gods. Then he explained that he

---

1. Sermon on Deuteronomy 5:22.

did not will to be represented by images or grotesque figures, since he is spirit and wishes to be served spiritually by us. For men ought not go about setting up just anything, but God wants to have a spiritual service. He wants his name to be hallowed; he wants us to practice his work and, above all, so to forbear that we each disavow our thoughts and affections to the extent that we might experience a reprieve in which God can govern us. That is what this first table of the law contains. As for the second, we have seen that he commanded us to honor our father and mother [and] forbade us to murder, commit adultery, steal, lie, and covet. That is why God divided his law into two tables.

Accordingly, if we seriously want to regulate our life, let us continually maintain the intention to honor our God and then to live with our neighbors in complete justice and equity. For there are some who refrain from doing evil but who nevertheless rarely think of God and who consider themselves free and absolved, provided no one complains against them in this world. Yet I ask you, what is this? For as long as we aren't thieves, is it all right for us to be sacrilegious? Is it not a more heinous crime to ravish the honor of God than to rob a man, or to cut away his purse [or] pick the lock on his chest?

Consequently let us not suppose that we have done everything simply because others neither bring to trial nor direct a complaint against us, for it is a matter of God's having what he demands as well as his due. For we are obligated to pay him homage all our life. Therefore it is all the more incumbent on us to direct our study toward observing the first table of the law, that we might not lead a philosophical life as pagans do in our effort to live honestly with men, but may God's honor be our most precious concern and our starting point.

FRANCIS I (1494–1547)

King of France. Calvin dedicated his *Institutes* to Francis I, but the king proved to be an enemy of Christ and persecutor of His church.

45

Making Our Responsibility Clear[1]

"And they called them, and commanded them
not to speak at all nor teach in the name of Jesus.
But Peter and John answered and said unto them,
Whether it be right in the sight of God to hearken
unto you more than unto God, judge ye."

—Acts 4:18–19

The apostles point us to the road we must follow.
That is, we must withstand the threats and the exalted
position of men and not waver in our duty. We must
take a stand and faithfully fulfill what God demands
of us, even when it would appear that those who
exercise authority over us have the right to enjoin
us to forgo proclaiming and supporting our Master's
cause. We must realize that they do not, for he honors
us by calling us for that very purpose. Now in order to
do this, we must be grounded in the knowledge that
throughout our lives we are to endeavor to follow
God's commands, for it is he who guides and directs
us in everything we do. It is true men are able to
impose laws on us, as is the custom of princes, kings,
and magistrates, who are in authority over others, but
those laws are also to guide us and direct us to God.

---

1. Sermon on Acts 4:16, 18–19.

In all this, however, our Lord always reserves sovereignty for himself. When establishing princes and magistrates, he does so not to diminish his honor or relinquish his right but to be honored by them in their position. They are to rule in his stead. They are his lieutenants, as it were, because all the world's principalities and dominions are subject to him. In the same way that a sergeant or an officer of the law is subject to the judge and under his authority and does nothing without the authority of his superior, so princes and magistrates, however great, must attempt nothing against the will of God, nor can they. The prevailing general rule is that God must govern us.

However, we must equally note that whatever office we occupy, our Lord makes our responsibility clear. There is a general rule that he sets before all the faithful. It is that law that contains the Ten Commandments. Beyond that, he declares to each officeholder his responsibility in the context of his calling. If a man has the authority to direct and govern others, the Word of God shows him why he has been elevated to that position and how he must comport himself in it. The same is true for all officeholders. Our Lord will make it clear to a wicked man what he must do. Likewise, a man of low estate will be instructed concerning his duty. It is true that those who have resisted him all their lives have the notion that they are not obliged to obey in any way whatsoever. They have such contempt for God and his Word that they adamantly refuse to submit to his will. As for the faithful, on the other hand, God will not permit them to rise up against him, because they present themselves to him with humility so that he may govern them. It is as I have said before. We must not presume to set up anything that contravenes God's teaching. As soon as he makes clear what his will is, we must follow where he leads. Do we understand that?

Guillaume Farel's last visit with Calvin
on his deathbed.

Recommended Books
by or about Calvin

Life of Calvin

The Life of John Calvin – Theodore Beza (Banner of Truth)

John Calvin – Simonetta Carr (for children; Reformation Heritage)

The Man God Mastered – Jean Cadier (IVF)

A Life of John Calvin: A Study in the Shaping of Western Culture – Alister E. McGrath (Blackwell)

John Calvin: A Biography – T. H. L. Parker (Westminster Press)

Portrait of Calvin – T. H. L. Parker (SCM Press)

John Calvin: His Life and Influence – Robert Reymond (Christian Focus)

John Calvin: A Pilgrim's Life – Herman J. Selderhuis (IVP)

Calvin – Emanuel Stickelberger (James Clarke)

This was John Calvin – Thea Van Halsema (Baker)

John Calvin: Biography and Theology – Willem van 't Spijker (Westminster John Knox)

John Calvin – Williston Walker (Christian Focus)

Calvin: The Origins and Development of His Religious Thought – Francois Wendel (Collins)

Writings by Calvin (other than sermons)

The Bondage and Liberation of the Will (Baker)

Calvin's Ecclesiastical Advice (T. & T. Clark)
Commentaries (Baker, 22 vols.)
Concerning the Eternal Predestination of God –
    ed. J. K.S. Reid (James Clarke)
Concerning Scandals (Eerdmans)
Golden Booklet of the True Christian Life (Baker)
Institutes of the Christian Religion–McNeill/Battles
    edition (Westminster Press, 2 vols.)
John Calvin: Writings on Pastoral Piety – ed. Elsie Ann
    McKee (Paulist Press)
Letters of John Calvin (Banner of Truth)
The Necessity of Reforming the Church (Protestant
    Heritage Press)
*The Piety of John Calvin: An Anthology Illustrative of the
    Spirituality of the Reformer* – ed. Fred Klooster
    (Baker)
On Prayer: Conversation with God – ed. I. John Hesselink
    (Westminster John Knox)
Tracts and Letters – ed. Henry Beveridge and Jules
    Bonnet (Baker, 7 vols.)
Treatises on the Sacraments (Reformation Heritage
    and Christian Focus)

Sermons by Calvin
The Mystery of Godliness (Eerdmans)
Sermons on Acts chapters 1-7 (Banner of Truth)
Sermons on the Beatitudes (Banner of Truth)
Sermons on the Death and Passion of Christ (James Clarke)
Sermons on the Deity of Christ (Old Paths)
Sermons on Deuteronomy (Banner of Truth)
Sermons on Election and Reprobation (Old Paths)
Sermons on Ephesians (Banner of Truth)
Sermons on Galatians (Banner of Truth)

Sermons on Job (Banner of Truth)
Sermons on Melchizedek and Abraham (Old Paths)
Sermons on Micah (P & R)
Sermons on Psalm 119 (Old Paths)
Sermons on 2 Samuel (Banner of Truth)
Sermons on the Saving Work of Christ (Eerdmans)
Sermons on the Ten Commandments (Baker)
Sermons on Timothy and Titus (Banner of Truth)
Songs of the Nativity: Selected Sermons on Luke 1 & 2
    (Banner of Truth)

Daily Readings and Quotables from Calvin

365 Days with Calvin— ed. Joel R. Beeke (Reformation
    Heritage/Day One)
Calvin's Wisdom: An Anthology – Graham Miller
    (Banner of Truth)
Day by Day with John Calvin (Hendrickson)
This is My Heart: Devotional Readings (Reformation
    Heritage)
*Grace and its Fruits: Selections from Calvin on the Pastoral
    Epistles* (Evangelical Press)

Selected Studies on Calvin

Analysis of the Institutes – Ford Lewis Battles
    (P & R)
Interpreting John Calvin – Ford Lewis Battles (Baker)
*What Calvin Says: An Introduction to the Theology of John
    Calvin* – Gary Crampton (Trinity Foundation)
Calvin and the Biblical Languages – John Currid
    (Christian Focus)
Let Christ Be Magnified: Calvin's Teaching for Today –
    J. H. Merle d'Aubigne (Banner of Truth)

The Writings of John Calvin: An Introductory Guide –
ed. Wulfert de Greef (Baker)

The Knowledge of God in Calvin's Theology – Edward
Dowey (Eerdmans)

Calvin's Christology – Stephen Edmonson (Cambridge)

Calvin and the Sabbath – Richard Gaffin (Christian
Focus)

*Articles on Calvin and Calvinism: A Fourteen-Volume
Anthology of Scholarly Articles* – ed. Richard C.
Gamble (Garland)

John Calvin and the Church: A Prism of Reform –
ed. Timothy George (Westminster John Knox)

Calvin's Concept of the Law – I. John Hesselink
(Pickwick)

Calvin's First Catechism – I. John Hesselink (Westminster John Knox)

The Christian Polity of John Calvin – Harro Höpfl (Cambridge University Press)

Calvin's Doctrine of the Work of Christ – John Frederick
Jansen (James Clark)

Calvin's Doctrine of Predestination – Fred Klooster (Baker)

John Calvin: Student of the Church Fathers – Anthony
Lane (Baker)

The Expository Genius of John Calvin – Steven J. Lawson
(Reformation Trust)

John Calvin's Doctrine of the Christian Life – John H. Leith
(Westminster Press)

The Cambridge Companion to John Calvin – ed. Donald
K. McKim (Cambridge University Press)

Calvin's Doctrine of the Church – Benjamin C. Milner, Jr.
(Brill)

Calvin's Geneva – William Monter (Wiley)

The Unaccommodated Calvin: Studies in the Foundation

of a Theological Traditions – Richard A. Muller
(Oxford University Press)

The Theology of Calvin – Wilhelm Niesel
(Lutterworth Press)

Calvin: An Introduction to His Thought – T. H. L. Parker
(Westminster John Knox Press)

Calvin's New Testament Commentaries – T. H. L. Parker
(T. & T. Clark)

Calvin's Old Testament Commentaries – T. H. L. Parker
(T. & T. Clark)

Calvin's Preaching – T. H. L. Parker (T. & T. Clark)

John Calvin: A Heart for Devotion, Doctrine, and Doxology
– ed. Burk Parsons (Reformation Trust)

John Calvin and His Passion for the Majesty of God –
John Piper (Crossway)

Calvin and the Atonement – Robert Peterson (Christian
Focus)

Calvin's Doctrine of the Last Things – Heinrich Quistorp
(John Knox Press)

The Spirituality of John Calvin – Lucien Richard
(John Knox Press)

Calvin Handbook – ed. Herman J. Selderhuis
(Eerdmans)

Calvin's Theology of the Psalms – Herman J. Selderhuis
(Baker)

*The Nature and Function of Faith in the Theology of John
Calvin* – Victor Shepherd (Mercer University Press)

Calvin in Context – David Steinmetz (Oxford University
Press)

Calvin's Teaching on Job – Derek Thomas (Christian
Focus)

Christ in Our Place: The Substitutionary Character of

Calvin's Doctrine of Reconciliation – Paul Van Buren (Eerdmans)

Calvin, Geneva and the Reformation – Ronald S. Wallace (Baker)

Calvin's Doctrine of the Christian Life – Ronald S. Wallace (Oliver & Boyd)

Calvin's Doctrine of the Word and Sacraments – Ronald S. Wallace (Oliver & Boyd)

Calvin and Calvinism – B. B. Warfield (Baker, Vol. V of *Works*)

Influence

Living for God's Glory: An Introduction to Calvinism – Joel R. Beeke (Reformation Trust)

The Quest for Full Assurance: The Legacy of Calvin and His Successors – Joel R. Beeke (Banner of Truth)

Reformed Confessions Harmonized – ed. Joel R. Beeke and Sinclair B. Ferguson (Baker)

The Reception of Calvinistic Thought in England – Charles D. Cremeans (University of Illinois Press)

History of the Reformation in Europe in the Time of Calvin (8 vols. in 4) – Jean Merle d'Aubigne (Sprinkle)

Reformed Confessions of the 16th and 17th Centuries in English Translation – James Dennison (Reformation Heritage Books)

Calvinism in Europe, 1540–1620 – ed. Alastair Duke, Gillian Lewis, and Andrew Pettegree (Manchester University Press)

Later Calvinism: International Perspectives – ed. W. Fred Graham (Sixteenth Century Journal Publishers)

Calvin and the Calvinists – Paul Helm (Banner of Truth)

John Calvin: Contemporary Prophet – ed. Jacob Hoogstra (Eerdmans)

The Emergence of Liberty in the Modern World: The Influence of Calvin – Douglas Kelly (Presbyterian and Reformed)

Calvinism in History: A Political, Moral, and Evangelizing Force – Neil McFetridge (Solid Ground)

The History and Character of Calvinism – John T. McNeill (Oxford University Press)

After Calvin: Studies in the Development of a Theological Tradition – Richard Muller (Oxford)

Christ and the Decrees: Christology and Predestination in Reformed Theology from Calvin to Perkins – Richard A. Muller (Baker)

Post-Reformation Reformed Dogmatics – Richard A. Muller (Baker, 4 vols.)

Calvinism on the Frontier 1600–1660: International Calvinism and the Reformed Church in Hungary and Transylvania – Graeme Murdock (Oxford University Press)

Calvin and the Consolidation of the Reformation – William G. Naphy (Manchester University Press)

International Calvinism, 1541–1715 – ed. Menna Prestwich (Clarendon Press)

John Calvin: His Influence in the Western World – W. Stanford Reid (Zondervan)

Civic Calvinism in Northwestern Germany and the Netherlands: Sixteenth to Nineteenth Centuries – Heinz Schilling (Sixteenth Century Journal Publishers)

Calviana: Ideas and Influence of John Calvin – ed. Robert V. Schnucker (Sixteenth Century Journal Publishing)

John Calvin: His Roots and Fruits – C. Gregg Singer (A Press)

Reformers in the Wings – David C. Steinmetz (Oxford University Press)

Puritans and Calvinism – Peter Toon (Reiner)

Reformed Theology in America – ed. David Wells (Baker)

Bibliographies

For an annotated bibliographical guide to Calvin's vast corpus and material on his life and theology printed prior to 1964, see Lester de Koster, "Living Themes in the Thought of John Calvin: A Bibliographical Study" (Ph.D. dissertation, University of Michigan, 1964). For bibliography on Calvin and Calvinism since the 1960s, see Peter De Klerk and Paul Field's annual articles in the *Calvin Theological Journal.* See also D. Kempff, *A Bibliography of Calvinism, 1959–1974* (Potchefstroom: I. A. C., 1975), and Michael Bihary, ed., *Bibliographia Calviniana* (Prague: n.p., 2000). The best list of Calvin and Calvinism resources is available from the database of the Henry Meeter Center, Calvin College Library, Grand Rapids, Michigan (www.calvin.edu/meeter).